THE LITTLE ASCENSION HANDBOOK

Guidelines from the Universe for Your
Spiritual Journey to Wholeness

Christine Barclay

BALBOA.PRESS
A DIVISION OF HAY HOUSE

Balboa Press books may be ordered through booksellers or by contacting:

Balboa Press
A Division of Hay House
1663 Liberty Drive
Bloomington, IN 47403
www.balboapress.com.au
1 (877) 407-4847

Because of the dynamic nature of the Internet, any web addresses or links contained in this book may have changed since publication and may no longer be valid. The views expressed in this work are solely those of the author and do not necessarily reflect the views of the publisher, and the publisher hereby disclaims any responsibility for them.

The author of this book does not dispense medical advice or prescribe the use of any technique as a form of treatment for physical, emotional, or medical problems without the advice of a physician, either directly or indirectly. The intent of the author is only to offer information of a general nature to help you in your quest for emotional and spiritual well-being. In the event you use any of the information in this book for yourself, which is your constitutional right, the author and the publisher assume no responsibility for your actions.

Any people depicted in stock imagery provided by Getty Images are models, and such images are being used for illustrative purposes only. Certain stock imagery © Getty Images.

Print information available on the last page.

ISBN: 978-1-5043-1998-0 (hc)
ISBN: 978-1-5043-1996-6 (sc)
ISBN: 978-1-5043-1997-3 (e)

Balboa Press rev. date: 12/30/2019

Contents

Introduction

This is a handbook. A handbook is a reference book that breaks down a larger topic in order to give you short explanations about its various aspects. It gathers together from many detailed sources the information people need to get started. It gives the full range of subtopics in brief which will allow you to

a) know that such a thing does exist with reference to the overall topic,

b) select the areas that are of greater interest or need from the range given, and

c) research further to assist you in obtaining greater knowledge.

The greater topic is your spiritual awakening, your enlightenment, your ascension to the life that your soul was always meant to live.

This is perhaps the most important area of knowledge for anyone to delve into. And because you are reading this, you know that the information is vital to your well-being and progress. On my own spiritual journey I have explored so many avenues of information that were linked to my understanding of this process. Like Alice going down the proverbial rabbit hole, I have been led off in multiple directions. I have been shocked and appalled at some revelations, and comforted and elevated with others. Each of the items of information I have discovered have been part of my journey so far, and there is still so much more for all of us to explore as people awaken across the world and need to learn new ways of doing things.

My objective in writing this book is to provide you with a list of basic explanations about these spiritual topics. I hope that it helps you to understand enlightenment and ascension, which is sometimes called transcendence. There are many parts to the big picture, and after reading this, you can focus on those that particularly interest you. This book gives you the broad overview. Everything you investigate during your spiritual awakening will eventually lead you to the desired outcome, and the route you choose will be the best one for you, as you are on this journey of understanding and will do things the way that is right for you.

Understand that this is *your* journey, and while there may be many people who are your guides and teachers, the responsibility will always be yours to fact check, research further, and ensure that the knowledge resonates as truth for you. Go within and ask yourself if the information will fit into your world concept.

But also try to suspend judgement. We often read something and reject it immediately because that fact doesn't fit in with our currently accepted world view. We can go into what is called cognitive dissonance, where what we read is too far away from what we know right now, and so our initial judgement is that it is a lie; it's too hard to believe. There have been many examples of this throughout history; what people thought was impossible at that moment turned out to be the eventual truth. Think about the concepts of motorised flight or space travel when they were first tried. Many people wouldn't believe it until they saw it for themselves, but it was happening.

So, enjoy your trip. Read this handbook a few times and think about the questions I have asked; are these the ones you are asking yourself and maybe have been for a long time? Talk about these things with your friends; they might be on their spiritual journey too.

Above all, don't just take my word for it; investigate everything I say. There is a wealth of knowledge out there that is available for you to dip into. Use this handbook as the starting point for your journey of discovery. Add notes to it, make it a true record of your learning, and keep it with you.

My focus has been a positive one. There are some things happening in the world today that are frightening and unacceptable, and you will no doubt discover these as you investigate. Face that darkness but try not to let it overwhelm you. Know that it exists, that it should not exist, and that we want to stop it from existing by living in a better way as human spirits.

Send your love not only to those who are being hurt, but also to the ones who are doing the hurting as they are spirits as well. You might go into the depths of despair and feel anger and shock, and perhaps the bitterness of betrayal when you find out that some of those that you idolised are not who you thought they were. But work through it; you will come out on the other side with knowledge and understanding that will help you to forge your way to a better world for all of us.

Bless you, and happy learning.

CHAPTER 1

Who Am I?

All about You: The Quick Version

You are a spirit having a human experience, a divine soul currently on Earth to experience life.

Like everything else in the universe, you are energy and connected to all that is energy—the totality of existence, in fact.

You are here right now because you made a decision—a contract—to be human and learn lessons to perfect your soul. You will return your experience to the Source.

You are here on Planet Earth, but what you see with your human eyes isn't everything there is to see. In fact, it is an illusion that is shared by all living things.

?

You learn. Learn about everything and love. Learn how to love everyone, no matter what.

You Are a Spirit

> They were partly correct. You are actually a spirit with a human body, having a human experience. The essence of you is your spirit. It is the true you, the energetic you, the one that goes on forever. Our souls never die. We just change focus. We take every lifetime's experience with us. Every lifetime builds wisdom and has particular lessons for us to learn.

Your Higher Self

Your higher self (HS) has a direct connection with the Source, and it knows what you consciously know as well as what you have yet to discover about yourself.

It keeps track of all the lessons you have learned over your lifetimes, and it helps you to continue this learning by bringing into your life people and events that enable you to show your improvement. You may be relatively young as you read this book right now, but you have probably been here a few times already and just don't remember.

It is a good idea to ask your higher self to help you understand the important lessons for you to learn. How do you do this? Your HS may not be a loud voice in your head, but it is always present, watching and guiding you. It will be a quiet, insistent messenger saying the same thing a few times. It may even give you a physical prompt in some way. Listen to it. Make a habit of listening to it and doing what it says. Try asking your HS what is for your highest good to do that day or what lesson will you be able to complete. This will give you a focus of expectation for learning. When you have asked and found the answer, then somehow life is more settled and fulfilling; you feel more prepared for what might come your way during your day. The experiences that are the most helpful for the evolution of your consciousness come in a sequence, and when you handle them with an aware mind as much detached from drama and emotion as possible, they enable you to become a better person.

Our Consciousness Levels

Humans have great potential to expand their consciousness and become awake and alive to all the possibilities that there are in the universe.

To do this, your heart must awaken to those possibilities, and courage and persistence must be shown to get to the greatest expression of your ideals. There are levels of awareness that you go through during your life as you realise the purpose you have here as part of your spiritual journey. These consciousness levels are not all experienced by everyone. It is not necessarily true that it takes chronological maturity to reach the highest, as some children are more advanced than adults in this respect.

Level of Consciousness	Explanation
Survival Mode	• You seek safety from danger, and in this stage, fear dominates your life. • Your default position is not to trust. It is to suspect others, wanting something but not truly believing that you deserve it or even that it is possible for you to get. • Because you don't trust others, you see them as competing with you, and you may try to exploit them as you are without the empathy and compassion to treat them as you want to be treated. • You think that as you don't deserve wonder and joy, others don't deserve them either. This level is very much about the frightened self, living in fear and lack.
Connecting with Others	• You reach out to others. Some of your relationships result in pleasure and affirmation of your needs, and some in sorrow and disappointment, but you *are* making a connection. This could be a romantic relationship or one of family or friendship. You put yourself out there and become vulnerable to misunderstanding or you enable love to happen. • You may experience pain or joy, and you do this through interaction, giving to and taking from others.

Controlling Others	• You seek to control yourself and others. You may have rules and regulations that you live by that give you a sense of order and well-being. • At times, you try to apply these rules to others, usually thinking lots of 'shoulds' that others must abide by. For example, *They should listen when I tell them something* or *They should not do it that way.* • When other people don't comply with your wishes, you are annoyed and angry at them. You believe it is their duty to do it your way and that they should relinquish their own personal power to your will. You know best. • This level is not entirely negative, as wanting to have order in your life is not inherently bad. When you try to impose these strictures onto others, and they do not want them, there may become a problem of domination, taking away another person's free will and ability to decide.
Serving Others	• This highest level of awareness is an awakening from the lower three levels. • Sometimes, you move between these levels in your interactions with others, feeling emotions and trying to rise to a higher way of being. • You can see the imperfections of yourself, of others, of relationships, of events, of all these things, yet you accept them unconditionally, without judgement, and through the filter of love. • Being aware does not mean that you are perfect, as you are still human and subject to the stress of interaction and the impact of your emotions. • Being aware means that you understand and you try your best to remain in that state of love and service.

When you are at the highest level of awareness, you can't help but love others. Even when they don't love you back, even when they try to hurt you, you have the will to treat them with kindness and respect, to show them empathy and compassion whatever they do or say. It's difficult to look at someone who has done what others consider an evil deed and accept them without judgement. To look past the deed to the person and love that person is surely a high state consciousness.

To look at the people you meet every day and know that they have their struggles and may not be at their best all the time, is to show love. Trying to understand the failings of others is to show love. Forgiving and acknowledging their goodness, even when they have caused you pain, is to show love.

Your Three Minds

We have three minds. Each has a certain function and deals with various aspects of your life and your existence within three-dimensional reality. Each operates within a brainwave frequency spectrum and has a relationship to time itself.

Name of Mind	What Kind of Mind Is It?	What Are Its Time Parameters?	What Kind of Brainwaves Does It Use?
Conscious	• analytical and intellectualised • your thinking mind • rational and logical • holds information in short-term memory	operates in the past and the future, with reference to the present	beta frequency brainwaves
Subconscious	• unlimited storage capacity—a super processor • beliefs, memories, life experiences, and the interpretation of them; emotions and hopes are kept here	always in the present moment	alpha and theta frequency brainwaves

Unconscious	• governs autonomic body systems • home of higher self, spiritual connections, and access to collective unconscious	always in the present moment	delta wave frequency spectrum

The subconscious and the unconscious minds are often classed together, and both can be accessed through meditation and other techniques, if you seek to make changes in the way you think.

The subconscious operates with a set of rules designed to protect your well-being—a kind of ego defence mechanism. It governs your personality development and your personal growth. This mind guides you to act instinctively within the parameters of your ethical and moral values, and the programming you experienced when you were in your formative years, from before birth until six or seven years old.

The subconscious can cause a physical and emotional reaction to a thought because the pattern for such reactions was set in the past, when you experienced a similar event. The feelings you had in that first instance will recur, sometimes sending you back into the memory of the initial event, including the emotional charge. The recall capacity of our subconscious memory is perfect, but that of the conscious mind is not. This can be seen when people are put into a hypnotic state and are asked to recall and describe an event that their conscious mind may have no recollection of.

The subconscious practices homeostasis not only for the body, but also to keep your mind, your attitudes, and your actions consistent with what you did in the past. So that you stay in your comfort zone and continue with your habitual thinking patterns, your subconscious causes feelings of emotional and physical discomfort when you try to change or break habits. It does its best to keep you in the complacency of your familiar ways, and it takes a great deal of creativity and repetition to move from this into new patterns of thinking and behaviour.

The subconscious also does not differentiate between what you physically do and what you think about doing. That means that you can visualise exercising with as much detail, emotion, and focus as possible, and it is like you have done a real workout. This has been proven through programs used for training athletes to gain muscle memory. The subconscious can also stop time. If you are totally immersed in a favourite activity, time seems to stand still for you even though it passed normally in the outer world.

If you avoid using your conscious mind, operating automatically and without conscious thinking, the subconscious mind will step up and take over. This is a good way of finding out about how you feel about something, as prejudices, emotions, and even physical reactions will manifest, and you will be given an insight into your programming. These feelings will stay in place unless you make a conscious effort to replace them with better ways of reacting.

We can ask our subconscious to assist us as well, by framing a positive and specific question for it to work on during the day. Seemingly random events will occur that are related to answering that question. For example, you might ask, "How can I connect better with others?" in the morning as you wake, and your brainwaves are still in theta (meditative) state. And during the day, you will find many opportunities for conversations. You may have the chance to clear up some misunderstanding you have with another, and the chances for happy and positive talk will manifest so that you connect better with others.

Asking a question before napping or sleeping is another good practice. During our sleep, new synaptic connections are formed, and old ones are cleared up. Writing the question down will help you remember and keep a record. Einstein and Tesla were great believers in the power of naps, knowing that the conscious mind releases control, and the abundant field of consciousness that we are connected to is activated during that time.

Your Thoughts

Thoughts stream through our minds in an endless procession. They can be organically triggered through sensation or the remnants of conversations; be attached to strong emotions from an event or an interaction; or simply be random musings about any topic. If someone says, "Don't think about an elephant," then that is all you can think about.

Thoughts can be positive or negative or neutral, without any definable feeling. They can recur at any time and cannot always be squashed down when we want them to go away. They can be linked like carriages on a train, one to another (a train of thought), where you may not easily remember the original. You think all day long, and then your mind keeps you dreaming, sometimes incorporating the day's events into a little scenario, sometimes focusing on one image, often in a confusing way.

When thoughts are attached to emotions, they became powerful and memorable. At times, remembering something can bring the event back into this moment, with all the accompanying feelings. The emotion is what you really remember, because it is felt in the body, and it can also work the other way around, with an emotion triggering a pattern of thoughts.

Are thoughts important? Is thinking important? Yes, to both questions. However, the fact that we cannot control what pops into our minds leads us to the conclusion that we need some way of managing these thoughts.

What you focus on gains importance and power. So, if you idly think that you are hungry and then focus on the feeling, the lack of food and the fact that you haven't eaten for hours, then it will loom large in both your mind and your body. But let the thought of *hungry* drift through without focusing on it, and it will leave you alone until you finally eat. It is possible to gain some control over our thoughts this way. Flicking them away, thanking them for coming, and then ignoring them will make them obey to some extent.

When you practice meditation frequently, you will find that

you have fewer random thoughts, that your mind is more orderly, and that your focus on important things is better.

As we know that our thoughts create our reality, having this level of control is an extremely good thing. Thoughts as energy are manifested into reality. They are powerful, particularly when there is a collective gathering of the same thoughts. When many people meditate together and focus on peace and freedom, there is a measurable effect on the collective consciousness, shown in a reduction of violence in the world. If everyone changed their thoughts to having only peace and plenty in the world, no one would want war, and everyone would have what they need to live.

What you are today is a result of what you thought yesterday. What you will be tomorrow will be a consequence of what you are thinking today.

Your Intuition

Trust your intuition, as it opens doors to creativity, to higher guidance, and to clarity of understanding of the world and of yourself. Intuition is a right-brain function. To explain the nature of intuition is not easy; you simply know without knowing how you know. Intuitive decisions are aligned with your subconscious mission and your personal destiny, of which your conscious reasoning mind is unaware. The subconscious mind delivers symbolic images, colours, words, and tactile or kinaesthetic sensations, such as gut feelings, as a message to let you know that you are on the right track or to tell you that there is a problem of some sort.

When you trust your intuition, you tap into synchronous and seemingly magical elements of reality, accessing inner guidance and meeting opportunities that might have otherwise remained hidden. Intuition can be a happy accident, but it is possible for people to develop and perfect their intuitive powers. To develop mastery, let your conscious mind form a close and trusting relationship with your subconscious mind. You can find a way to access your subconscious through relaxation, meditation, deep breathing, chanting, and fasting.

If you ask the right questions, give a clear and focused request, and follow that with a state of relaxed receptivity and trust, the answer will come to you. It could be something that you hear, either out loud from another person or in your mind (clairaudience); something that you see physically or mentally (clairvoyance); or a strong positive or negative feeling (clairsentience). Intuitive messages can also come through when you are writing if you open yourself up to the guidance of universal consciousness. The vast storehouse of accumulated wisdom is always available to you though your intuitive connections with life.

Most of us can easily know who is on the phone without looking or be aware of what someone is going to say next. Moving your intuition to the next level will enable you to have a much closer connection with others, as we are all part of the field of energy that is consciousness.

The Heart and Love

As your heart awakens, your sense of separation and isolation begins to fade, and you will experience a variety of perceptual and behavioural shifts.

You will see yourself as being the only one there is. That seems selfish, but you are everyone, and everyone is you, so loving yourself is loving others. When you truly understand this concept and live it, you will lose your taste for competition. You will understand the need to survive and thrive together as a collective.

To live from your heart, place your attention there while speaking, listening, seeing, touching, and thinking. You can create amazing synchronicities that enrich your life by mindfully opening your heart and linking this awareness to the senses you use when interacting with the world. When you speak from your heart, spiritualising your senses, it creates a bridge of love and understanding between people. Connect your heart to your thoughts, and send healing wishes and blessings to yourself and others.

See from your heart the world of nature and humanity through eyes of wonder and love. Look into the eyes of others to see yourself. Listen from the heart without judgement, expectations, or opinions. Heal from the heart. Connect your heart to your voice, your thoughts, and your touch to help heal others.

Every soul is looking for happiness; seeking to avoid suffering; fighting their own battles with fear, insecurity, and self-doubt. They are searching for greater meaning, purpose, and connection. We are awakening to the truth that we are all in this world together as one.

What does this love look like? What kind of behaviours should we show to keep love alive? Use kind and complimentary words, withhold criticism, touch gently, show loyalty, express feelings in a positive way, say thank you and sorry, ask for and offer forgiveness, listen well, pay attention to others, and always have a sense of humour. Try to value and consider the needs of others, communicate well with them, and accept their imperfections as you do your own. Allow people to have their own interests and friendships, giving each other space and time, and sharing whatever you have. These behaviours can easily be part of your everyday interactions.

Your Emotions

When you were a baby, you expressed how you felt immediately, and when your needs were satisfied, you were happy again. Emotions were directly related to your bodily functions and your immediate environment. Nobody expected you to deny these feelings, as they were your way of communicating with others. You didn't hold onto any resentment, and you started fresh every moment. Emotions passed through you very quickly.

As you grew, you still felt the same things, but now people were telling you to tone your feelings down in the way they interacted with you. Suddenly, others were not as responsive as they once were, and you were denied what you wanted. Then when you began to interact through language, there were emotionally charged words to understand. There was more to deal with, and yet you were forced to repress how you felt. You quickly learned that showing some emotions was accepted, and other emotions were not appropriate. You were approved of when you were behaving in one way and rejected at other times. It is part of growing up and becoming an independent person; we all know that, but it is a hard lesson for us to learn, nevertheless.

As adults, we devalue our emotions every day. Reacting spontaneously is a rare thing, and we show our true selves only with our family or close friends. You would never dream of 'overreacting' with teachers or workmates, and you pay a physical price for this, with headaches, high blood pressure, insomnia, and so on. Your unexpressed emotions don't simply go away; they linger in your body and cause physical problems.

So, what generates these emotions? Your days are filled with interactions, and your mind is filled with thoughts. Your diet, the amount of quality sleep you get, what substances you are taking, your hormone levels, any illness or pain you are experiencing, your living circumstances and environment, memories that surface, associations you make with things or events, songs you hear, smells from the past: All manner of things trigger the full range of emotional responses. These are natural human reactions to the process of life. You are allowed to feel, and it is natural to feel.

The trick is to learn to express your feelings in productive ways. When strong emotions occur, it is a good idea to not react until you have had time to breathe and to think. Try to attend to your posture. Is your body tight? Are you starting to hold your breath? Endeavour to consciously relax your muscles; perhaps change your position or location, distract yourself by observing your surroundings, say something funny to take the edge off your strong feeling (maybe something like "Oh, well, these things happen.") If an immediate response is required, still take a moment to breathe and think, and then take the action that is appropriate.

If you feel hurt, allow the feeling. If you feel angry, allow that as well. Assertiveness training teaches us that we can say to the other person, "I feel angry because of what you said," or "What you did made me feel hurt." Own the feelings. Use "I feel ..." rather than "I am...," as this creates a distance between you and the emotion. Assertiveness is not being weak or rude; it is calling attention to the fact that you were affected by another person's words or actions. Of course, that person may not have the personal resources to react in an appropriate way, but you do. What they do is their reaction, and you only have control over yours. Letting others know that you have boundaries is healthy.

You can learn from your feelings. How you react emotionally to something or someone teaches you about yourself and helps you realise what it is you need to learn and practice to be a better person. Feel your feelings, but don't let them run your life. Be unattached to them; be like the baby you once were. Let them inside, and then let them go.

Your Ego

It is not always easy to keep yourself awake and aware. Many times, you slip up and go into an egoic state with your thoughts and interactions.

You dwell in the lower emotions as a result of the actions of others and rising into a more awakened state can be a slow and painful process. However, there are ways to keep you in the highest level, and they involve conscious words and deeds. Say kind and complimentary words to others; try to withhold criticism and frame your sentences with positive and encouraging words. Touch someone gently on the arm as you look into their eyes, smile a lot, always say thank you and sorry, actively listen when people speak with you, and use positive body language to show them your love.

Help people to lighten their load by holding the door open for them, making a funny remark, and giving them a smile. A brief loving interaction with someone may just save them from despair. Be the angel in the right place at the right time. All these actions take you away from yourself, out of your ego, and connect you with all of life.

Value others, actively considering what they may need, and try to provide that for them. Accept their imperfections as they accept yours; find out about their interests and offer friendship for the duration of the time you are with them. If you realise that people want to share something with you, make time and encourage them to have their say, counselling them to the best of your ability. Many times, people just want someone to listen to them.

It is important to know that you will not be perfect all the time. There may be people in your life who trigger the worst in you, and you may have to deal with them every day. This is a hard test for you, as you will be constantly challenged to be the better person. Forgiving and releasing (over and over) is the key. Try to move away from them emotionally and detach from the feelings they may bring to the surface. Look objectively at them and know that they too may be having their struggles with you. There is no need to be a friend. This person in your life has something to teach you (maybe patience), so try to learn that lesson, and demonstrate that you have learned it when you are tested. You will notice that they will interact less with you over time, and you will wonder why you were so upset with them.

Your Creative Potential

Everything is created twice: first in the mind, then in the material world. When someone imagines something, the process of that thing being brought into the physical begins. As humans, we have an innate sense of creativity, a great potential to bring forth new ideas for others to experience. We have created amazing art and literature. We have created machines and technology to enhance and enrich our lives. We have adapted and perfected the designs of others to streamline and improve them for our needs. It is innate in us as problem-solvers that we create.

From our earliest years, when we see patterns and colours, we emulate designs and create with images. We also create with words, both spoken and written, as we develop our language skills. Our minds are constantly creating, sometimes copying the works of others and sometimes with entirely original ideas. Our brains fire up, making neural connections that go into the shared memory in the field of consciousness. One of the major reasons for you to choose to come and experience human life is the potential for creating art or music or architecture or technology or developing more eco-friendly ways of living. Whenever there is a need, someone will create something to fill that need.

CHAPTER 2

What Am I Really?

The Field of Consciousness

Quantum physics and neuroscience have found that there exists a field of consciousness, of energy, that resides away from our physical brains but is interconnected in a way that allows learning and communication.

This energy field is part of what you use to function in the world, and you share it with all other sentient beings. It is a field of energy to which we are all connected, and this connection gives us shared access to all that there is. It is like the cloud, where a lot of computer information is now stored and accessed from.

The connection that this field of consciousness offers is unlimited. When you consciously focus on accessing this field, you can share all the information available. This information contains the accumulation of historical and scientific knowledge, and this is evidenced by the fact that when someone has made a discovery and haven't yet disclosed it, others seem to have discovered the same thing. That is because the thoughts and ideas were out there in the field of consciousness. Quantum entanglement occurred, with the knowledge available in the field, and so it is then accessed by people separated by distance.

The field can also provide confirmation of possibility; for example, after Roger Bannister ran the first four-minute mile in history, suddenly everyone (who wanted to) was able to do it. The notion of the field of conscious energy explains many coinciding events that have puzzled people for a long time.

Energy Is Everything

Everything—I mean everything—is energy. Matter is realised energy, and the whole universe is in energetic frequency vibration.

These vibrational frequencies differ according to the state of the matter, but it is all in motion. This energy is the same as light, the same as sound, the same as intelligence; it is consciousness. We are all points of consciousness in this vast sea of energy, and we are connected as a result of this.

The Newtonian (from Isaac Newton) science you learned in school makes the world into a clockwork model, where sensory perception is the only way of gathering evidence about the world, and the only things that are real are those that can be measured and quantified. According to Newtonian science, anything that you cannot see, feel, touch, taste, or smell does not exist, except in imagination and fantasies. Even emotions such as love are chemical reactions. Certainly, this way of understanding was a great start to explaining the world, but we know that there is so much more.

The science for today—quantum physics—confirms that solid matter does not exist in the universe and that all sentient beings share a field of conscious energy. Since the early 1900s, many scientists have revealed the truth about our world: that energy responds to consciousness, that one thing can affect another, even at a distance, through energetic interaction, and that everything that exists contains the information of everything else that exists, like a holographic plate that is broken into smaller pieces will always project the entire hologram and not just part of it.

Energy and Quantum States

Science is at the very beginning of exploring the subject of energy, and what is being discovered is what mystics have maintained over the millennia.

Quantum physics is confirming the fact that everything is energy. Quantum entanglement, where what happens to one particle affects the state of another particle, no matter how far apart they are, has applications in our lives, both spiritually and physically. These particles can vibrate in tune, regardless of the distance between them.

This means that we are all connected at the deepest level; it means that we can pull towards us the object of our desire, entwining our consciousness with it. Quantum superposition means that when not observed, a particle exists in all possible states of energy. When observed/thought of/desired, it moves into one state. This confirms that the sea of energy we are part of contains all variations of all that is, and when we focus on something, we bring it into being. Science is only now catching up to knowledge that has been in shared consciousness forever. It all proves that even your thoughts have an energetic effect on reality. Thinking creatively and positively will have a measurable effect on your life.

Energy and Your Body

We already know that our matter (body) is mostly water. And now, thanks to Dr Masaru Emoto's studies with water, we know that the vibrational frequencies of sound attached to a word (negative or positive in meaning) can have a profound effect on the molecules of water in our bodies. So, what is said to you and what you think must also affect you positively or negatively. You feel it in the fabric of your being. You internalise both self-talk and the words of others, and this can influence your physical and mental health. So, it follows that saying uplifting things to others and believing only positive and affirming things for yourself is crucial.

Energy: Light, Sound, and Healing

You can use energies such as light and sound to affect your health and wellness. There are many natural treatments available, along with a positive mental outlook, to regain health and not have to rely on a pharmaceutical fix. You are in charge; you have the power to keep yourself healthy and you have the responsibility to take care of yourself.

One example of sound healing is balancing your energy frequency through binaural beats. Remember that water (a large portion of our body's matter) is affected by sound, so sound can heal. Listening to Solfeggio tones directly affects your wellbeing as these tones resonate deep into your cells.

Being in the rays of the sun and in a natural environment has also proven to be healing and strengthening. It is said that for every illness, nature has provided a cure. Mother Gaia wants us to be healthy and happy, as we are part of her and part of the natural world itself. Balance and respect are the keys to wellness for all living creatures.

Because your body is made of energy, you can replenish spent energy by taking it from food. The sun provides the energy that enables food to grow (in the form of plants). The more your diet is plant-based, the closer the energy you take into your body is to the pure rays of the sun. You can also relax and replenish your energy through restful sleep and through creating, learning, and doing things that make you and others happy.

Energy Leaks

Ideally, your energies flow around and through you. But sometimes, there are obstructions and energy leaks. An energy leak is when you have anxiety or regret or fear or anger, or you feel unwell.

These leaks seem to suck away your well-being and cause you to feel tired and drained. You can also have blockages, be stuck in hatred for someone, or fear something and not be able to move on from that point. Sometimes, you can briefly distract yourself with thrill seeking, or physical and mental exertions, but you must try to deal with the issues behind blockages and discover why you fear this so much. Remember that the universe has your back. There is no need for fear or worry. Just relax into confident expectation that all is well. Keep your thoughts at a high vibrational level.

Monitor yourself to establish if you feel drained and tired around certain places (or even people) and try to avoid contact with them. It is important to take responsibility for your own well-being. Being proactive by speaking with that person to clear up any lingering issues that cause the anxiety is a positive move. Or it may be necessary to take a different job or relocate to a place where you feel clear and flowing energy.

Energy and Well-Being

When you are energetically cleared, you feel free, more joyful, and at peace with yourself and the world. The more you practice unblocking through re-energising your chakras and practicing forgiveness, the less the world affects your happiness.

You can remain in a state of bliss that is untouched by trouble, that is balanced and complete. This state of high energy frequency will have the great benefit of contributing to your overall health.

Think about when you have felt angry or depressed. These emotions can be accompanied by physical feelings of tightness, tiredness, or an upset stomach. Your blocked energy has caused you physical pain. Allowing the energy to flow, not being bothered by what others are doing or saying, and not being attached to any particular outcome will keep you in a state of flow and of joy (a wonderful place to be).

Your Energetic Connections to Others

Your energetic fields (your auras) are connected to all living things. Have you noticed animals, who are two-dimensional beings, greeting some people and rejecting others? Dogs are sensitive to energies and will respond positively to people they feel are welcoming and in an entirely different way to those they sense don't have good intentions (which the dog can sense in someone's energy frequency). Plants, which also have auras, will grow well for someone who projects love, plays them positive music, and talks to them. It is not just about water.

Sometimes, you can pass on energy to people who need it. They could be feeling overwhelmed by something happening in their lives, and a little boost from you is enough to return them to balance. So be generous with your hugs and your smiles. Giving energy away in small bursts does not deplete you, and continually checking yourself to monitor your own supply of energy will allow you to share your love with others freely. Replenish your own supply of energy through doing things that you love to do, taking a rest, meditating, and being around people who lift your spirits.

Your Chi

Chi is the vital life force of the universe. As we understand that energy is everything, we also know that it moves through our bodies along lines called meridians. The twelve meridians govern all areas of the body, including the organs and the circulatory system. There are points along the meridians, called acupuncture points, that access the energy flow for each organ. Chinese medicine has long used the notion that your chi is a major part of your ability to heal yourself and keep in a state of wellbeing.

Chi flows around the body, sometimes being blocked and causing problems that manifest in different areas. Consciously focus on bringing your energy back into a free flow state. If you have practiced a martial art or an energy healing system such as qigong or reiki, you recognise the energy flow of chi.

Your Chakras

Our human bodies have energy centres called chakras. *Chakra* is a Sanskrit word meaning "wheel," and the chakras spin like a wheel when they are working well, allowing energy to flow freely throughout our bodies.

You have seven chakras that are within your body and five more that link you to the Earth and to the celestial realms. When your chakras are blocked, it has a major effect on the way you feel physically and how you deal with others.

The chakras are associated with certain areas of your body; they have physical and emotional manifestations of imbalance, and these imbalances can be addressed by energising each out-of-balance chakra. For example, the *Muladhara* or root chakra, located at the base of the spine, governs your sense of safety, stability, and physical identity. If there is an imbalance, you could feel anxiety, have unfounded fears, or experience issues with your lower back and elimination organs, such as the bladder and colon.

Nutrition plays a part in helping your chakras function, as does the psychological effect of wearing symbols and colours for each of the chakras. There is a lot of information about chakras available online for you to investigate. It has been said that the optimal functioning of the three lower chakras in particular, the root, sacral, and solar plexus, is vital to give you the certainty of security, worth, acceptance, and feeling grounded and safe within your physical body and as a part of humanity.

Your Auras

As well as chakras, you have a whole series of layers to your aura, which is the energetic body surrounding you. Every living thing has an aura, and you can often pick up feelings through it about other people, even without speaking with them. There are seven layers, and each is connected to a chakra. The aura will be a colour, extending out from the body, and each layer will be higher in vibration than the one before it.

The first, called the Etheric, represents the basic fabric of your physical body. Then we have each layer—the Emotional (feelings), Mental (cognitive functions), Astral (links with others), Etheric Template (your overall physical blueprint), Celestial (connection to the Divine), and Ketheric, which is about a metre away from your body and connects you to the energetic universe through the crown chakra. Think about when you have stood near a person and felt comfortable or otherwise; your auras were mixing. As with the chakras, this is a very interesting energy topic to find out about, and there is a lot of information available.

We know that we all live in a sea of energy, a vibrational frequency, and we are conscious points of this energy. It is light, and because we are of this light, we are luminous. If you have ever seen a religious painting from earlier centuries, there is often a halo around the head of Jesus or one of the saints. This is their luminous aura, and such a phenomenon was readily accepted by the people of that time. What we would nowadays consider mystical and even magical is a true and valid thing.

Your Health and Healing

Energy therapies for healing are based on the idea that you are energy, which you know to be true. When your energy is out of balance, it can be returned to harmony by various practices that involve moving energy around the body and releasing it at the places where the energy has built up and is preventing a free flow, which is the state of well-being.

Reiki, one type of energy healing, targets the chakras and energy fields in and around your body where stagnation or blockages occur, causing illness and pain. The body's natural default state is wellness, so energy healing brings the body, mind, and spirit together in balance. When people have the intention of healing or being healed and trust in the process, they will be able to feel this energy as a sensation of warmth and tingling, moving throughout the body. There are many recorded instances of miraculous healings. It is not a miracle; it is the energetic solution to health always available to us.

When you subscribe to the idea that you are a powerful energy being, then you can heal yourself of minor and major ailments. You can avoid taking so many pharmaceuticals to relieve symptoms and aches and pains. Most of these medicines are allopathic. That is, they do not cure, they just relieve symptoms. This is not to say that doctors are no longer needed. It is a knowing that alternatives to the mainstream drugs and medical practices *can* be investigated and tried as a more natural and harmonious way to deal with the illness. A person in a state of balance and harmony may never actually become ill, as a high level of awareness and enlightenment will preclude any energy malfunctions.

Most of us are familiar with the idea of genetics, that the fabric of our bodies is governed by a set of criteria originating from our DNA. We have bought into the notion that our bodies are predisposed to be the way they are, as prescribed by that genetic encodement. However, as DNA is energy and part of the field of consciousness, then it follows that it is not the master enforcer of what we are, that there is another level of possibility above genetics. Dr Bruce Lipton coined the term *epigenetics*, which states that there is nothing hard and fast about DNA coding in that it will dictate our body responses. We *can* change and develop even the very fabric of our being. The environment we live in affects us to the very cellular level and the directed flow of positive consciousness that we actively use governs our health.

Gender and Sexuality

Embrace your sexuality and develop the capacity to enjoy intimacy with others. Society has overlaid this natural part of our human existence with a blanket of shame and guilt and embarrassment. We have been made to feel that sexual issues are rude, abnormal, and immoral.

Sometimes, simply growing up and going through puberty becomes unpleasant and shameful. The dilemmas and contradictions that all of us go through as part of maturing and entering adolescence become a trauma that is to be endured and repressed. Being a teenager is the link between childhood and adulthood, a bridge, so to speak, that must be crossed. There is no valid reason for shame or denial.

In our society, we seek to control sexuality or to flaunt it in a way that contributes to distorted understandings of it. You are asked by various authorities to abstain, to sublimate, to suppress your being, as if it is dirty and unmentionable. Our bodies need to be acknowledged. The processes we go through need to be accepted and affirmed. Otherwise, this leads to a kind of war between our body and our beliefs.

Sexuality has no inherent morality or immorality; it is just a process. We have put judgements and labels on it and sought to deny simple urges and class them as wrong. Cultural conditioning has led us to attach beliefs that are just that: not truth, not certainty, just someone else's belief. Sexual expression is an intimate, loving, and sacred act. Having it hijacked by cultural and religious mores, by advertising, by music and films has turned it into something that is exploitative and loveless.

There are also the gender stereotypes that our society has imposed upon us. We are expected to fulfil a role that is polarised and inflexible; it pits one against the other. The battle of the genders starts when we are children, as we are conditioned to be very girl or very boy through the way we are dressed, the toys we are given, the games we are encouraged to play, the way we are expected to participate in the running of the household, and how we are allowed to communicate (noisily and boy-like or quiet and reserved, like a girl).

This conditioning persists throughout our lives and takes its toll on our self-confidence, making us feel that our unique thoughts or feelings are wrong because they don't fit into what society wants. The battle of the genders takes its toll on our well-being as well. We intrinsically know that one gender is not better or worse than another, and yet throughout history, there has been a deliberate denigrating of women in terms of accepted roles in society, their ability to own property, their recognition as having equal intelligence and skill, and their overall capacity to contribute to the development of humanity. It has taken forceful efforts to redress this perception, and even now, there is residual belief in the lesser value of the female. We are all one; we are all male and female. We are all equally valuable and should all be equally valued.

CHAPTER 3

Where Am I?

Lady Gaia, Our Mother Earth

Gaia is the Earth, the Mother of all living beings. She is nature in its life-giving and nurturing aspect. Gaia is a goddess in some cultures, as she creates and sustains the Earth and all life on it. She is the embodiment of female power and force, as any life will fight to maintain and perpetuate itself.

Mother Earth is a self-regulating being, with all aspects of the planet—the temperature; the composition of the water, air, and land; the birth, life, and death of its creatures—all working in harmony. Or at least it was, until we humans began to exploit and destroy our very home as profit for a small minority. We now see that Gaia is out of balance, and she is seeking to return to her homeostasis. Like a dog shaking off fleas that are troubling it, Gaia is rumbling and shaking and reminding us all that our abuse is no longer acceptable.

Throughout recorded history and before, humans have given their children the legacy of a thriving planet. This has not been the case for the last few hundred years, as we have cut down forests, polluted water and land, ripped out minerals, and left scars on the Earth, all of these impacting the lives of all other living beings. We have a duty to ourselves and future generations to redress this imbalance and restore our beautiful mother to her former glory.

Treat Mother Earth as a treasured being, the source of all your life and the one that you truly belong to. Do things that show your respect; protest actions that continue to harm her and connect with her in gratitude for your very life.

The Sun and The Great Central Sun

As we know, our sun is the centre of our solar system. It creates life on our planet and, as energy, is part of us as well. This sun is not the only sun. Our sun is connected energetically to other suns in other galaxies and to the Great Central Sun.

The Great Central Sun is the heart centre of the cosmos and the point of integration of spirit and matter, the centre of the field of conscious energy that we are all part of.

Our own sun is ascending, along with Earth and all its creatures. As it ascends, it transmits to us the light codes it received from the source, which will help us in our own enlightenment and ascension. These light codes are pulses from the source, travelling multidimensionally and aiding us in our collective ascension back into oneness.

Try to sit in the sun with its warmth and light on your face and head for a short period of time each day; this will help you to receive these codes. The codes are helping us to rebirth into a higher place of existence; we are all ascending together. Some people are not aware of this yet, but they feel that something is happening. They know this because old systems and programs are starting to break down and become obsolete. When you are awake and aware, you can understand the best ways to ascend to this higher vibratory realm. Once we are all ascended into unity consciousness, we won't need governments and laws and religions any longer as we will all live in a system of love and respect, knowing that we are all one with our other selves.

Time

* Time is an illusion.
* Most of our energy particles exist in no time.
* This very moment is the only one there really is.

Your life is a series of linked moments, so the past, the present, and the future coexist. In the three-dimensional matrix, time was created to be part of the experience, but it is an artificial construct meant for the convenience of fitting things in at mutually known times, quantifying your days and your life. Time has become somewhat of an oppressor, making us feel that there is never enough of it, that we have no choice but to live and die by the clock. To gain for yourself a true feeling about time, and to return you to the place of no time, of zero point, where there is no rush or delay, meditation is the key.

All is happening in the now; there is no past or future. So logically, whatever it is that you project as doing later in your life has already been experienced. And whatever it was, you triumphed over any problems, sorted through the issues that needed to be dealt with, and you won.

So, relax and enjoy the moment. Use your knowledge of quantum entanglement to create a reality that is wondrous. Have the image in your mind of what you want; know that because time is a construct, and the past, the present, and the future are all there at the same moment, you already have what you want. Don't worry about what might happen; deal with what is happening now. And don't dwell on what has passed; you learned from it, and no amount of agonising over it can change it at all.

Earth Energy Lines

Earth energy lines or ley lines are lines of energy that coil around Mother Earth. The flow of energy, as in all parts of the universe, moves across the world, intersecting at various points. Some lines mark the positions of astronomical constellations as seen from Earth and many civilisations have built significant structures there: Stonehenge, the Pyramids, and Angkor Wat, to name just a few. The Earth also has energy points or chakras (just as our bodies do) on intersecting points, these being marked by natural or human-made monuments. There are maps that show the chakras of the world and many people feel an urge to visit these places to experience the energies.

Tracks and roads often follow ley lines (dragon lines, spirit lines, and dream lines, respectively, in China, South America, and Australia). Knowledge of ley lines has been around since ancient times; many studies have been done to measure the electromagnetic currents along the lines and at the points of intersection and these have shown the extent of energy movement.

Grounding and Earthing

Grounding or earthing refers to having direct contact with the surface of the Earth. This can be done by walking barefoot, by working in a garden and touching the soil, and by being out in nature and connecting with the Earth. When you directly contact the ground, you receive an energy charge that can boost your own energy reserves and also help you to sleep. It can also diminish pain, fatigue, and stress. You know how refreshing it is to go for a walk on a green lawn, or through a garden, in a forest, or along a beach. When you walk without shoes on, the electrons that are naturally coursing through the ground are accessed through your skin. These provide a boost to our own energy reserves.

In your daily life, you are disconnected from the Earth because of the synthetic shoes you wear, your artificial furnishings, and the asphalt and tar on the roads. You are also surrounded by and sometimes permeated by unnatural radiation from cell towers and

Wi-Fi signals. All these conveniences block the natural energies of the Earth, which you need to live well and feel well.

So, swim in a lake, do some gardening, lay on the ground, wear natural products rather than synthetic ones, go for walks near trees and on beaches. Simply touch the ground as much as you can and reconnect with Mother Earth.

Nature Deserves Our Reverence

We should always be mindful that we are part of the web of life on Earth. The Earth itself is the source of all our life and showing appropriate reverence and gratitude for this is vital. The air, water, food, and materials provided to us through our interactions with Mother Earth have sustained all the living creatures here since the beginning of time.

However, humankind has had a substantial negative impact in the last several decades so that we see a depletion of resources, extinction of species, and seemingly irreversible land and water damage caused by our actions. Thankfully, many people are actively aware of this and have alerted the rest of us. A movement has begun to repair and replenish the globe, and thus to live in a more harmonious way with the other inhabitants of the planet. But we should do a lot more.

As humans, we must acknowledge the rights of other species to exist, demonstrate that we wish them well through our actions in stopping their destruction and that of their environments, and improve their lives by replanting and safeguarding habitats. How can we do this?

- protect biodiversity by allowing all species to thrive (even weeds and insects)
- dispose of toxic substances so that minimal effects are experienced
- choose eco-friendly products

- grow food organically
- buy local and seasonal so that your ecological footprint is reduced
- recycle, reuse, and repurpose: all ways that you can incorporate respect for nature in your daily life

Buy products second-hand so that new ones don't always need to be made. Getting away from the idea of consumerism is a sound mind-set for the new Earth. Using renewable energy sources for the home and in our vehicles will collectively focus our thoughts on the well-being and health of all our natural systems. Be present in the natural world as often as you can so that your spirit is healed and put into a better balance.

Don't just know that you are part of the Earth; live in that way.

Sacredness

Something that is sacred is set apart and considered worthy of respect and reverence. The word can be applied to beliefs, practices, items, writings, songs, and sometimes people. A follower of a creed or religion will automatically hold as sacred the things that are held that way by most of the believers. There can also be sacredness that is personal to us. We can assign this notion to something that we cherish, to a quality that we hold above all others, such as trust, to commonly held beliefs such as human or animal rights, and to places we love.

Set aside time and space to discover what is sacred to you, asking yourself what you want to commit to or protect. This then becomes a focus for your attention and a thing of value in your life that you will guard and care for and possibly spread knowledge of to others.

The Schumann Resonance

The Schumann resonance is the electromagnetic rhythm of the Earth; it's the resonant frequency, or state of vibration, of the space between the surface of the Earth and the ionosphere. The number and severity of thunderstorms within this layer form part of the measurement, as these add electromagnetic energy. As well as this, the brain waves, biorhythms, and state of consciousness of all life forms contribute to these frequency readings. The pulses act as a background frequency that directly influences our nervous system; in some ways, it's like a heartbeat. Some people call it the heartbeat of the Earth.

The frequency of this resonance was set at a base level of 7.83 Hz when it was discovered by a German physicist in 1952. Recently, it has periodically risen dramatically to 40 Hz and higher. This has created a rise in consciousness amongst humans, and this is reflected in our questioning of what is happening in the world and our efforts to make it a better place for all life forms to live. We are starting to operate in a more aware and loving way and see systems that reflect this awareness. It is possible to see the Schumann Resonance readings daily and to get an overview of the energies that are always moving around us.

Atlantis, Lemuria and Mu

The belief in the idea of Atlantis, Lemuria, Mu, and other lost civilisations is conditional upon your willingness to accept that we don't know all there is to know about Earth and history; that truth is sometimes hidden. Atlantis has been mentioned throughout history, particularly by the Greek philosopher Plato around 360 BC; it was even drawn on a map in 1669. People still strongly believe in Atlantis, which asks us to question why this is such a prominent idea in our shared consciousness.

Atlantis, Lemuria, and Mu existed at different times and in

different places around the Earth. All of these were utopian societies advanced in understanding, wisdom, and technology. They were lost during natural cataclysms, and speculation exists that they were a series of experiments in civilisation and enlightenment. They existed at their highest levels of love and peace, and then discord entered, and they were destroyed. But their memory lives on in our shared consciousness.

CHAPTER 4

Why Am I Here?

Your Soul Contract

T hink about a story; it tells how a group of characters interacts in any given time and place. The story can have elements of comedy or tragedy; it can talk about pain and regret and love and all the life events we face. At any moment, anything can happen. The central characters can make a choice that takes them off in one direction, but if a different choice had been made, the story would have been totally changed.

When you read a story, you are a passive observer; the story is as the author wrote it. The events are set by the writer, and the action and interaction happen from there. But what if you had control over this story?

This is your story, the one that you are living now. You are not an observer, you are the author, the shaper, the one who can make it happen the way you want to happen. So, you can be who you want to be and do what you want to do. Does that sound a little crazy? Surely, events happen *to* a person.

But did you know that before you came to this planet, you decided which experiences you wanted and which lessons you wanted to learn? Which parents and family and nationality and time: everything about your story. Your energetic spirit made these decisions because there were some lessons for it to learn. For example, if you wanted to understand how to overcome helplessness, you may have chosen to have a disability and live with an unsupportive family, having difficulty accessing services to help you. Perhaps you chose to live in a culture that discriminated against those less able.

You had the opportunity to grow in strength of will, to learn to rely on yourself, to find your own support, to overcome the obstacles placed in your path. You learned your lesson well. At the end of the story, the end of your earthly life, you look back on the chapters and see your development, your failures and your successes, the way you loved others despite their denial of you, the way you learned to forgive them because you could see that they were learning their lessons as well. Maybe they succeeded; maybe they failed. But their story was their own.

The circumstances of your life were planned by your higher self and the spirits of your prospective family. Everyone agreed to the incarnation. Then, when the time was right, you were born into that family. Everyone, including you, went through the veil of forgetfulness. This is something we all do so that we start fresh in each new incarnation, experiencing free will, and having the opportunity to learn the lessons we have chosen to learn.

Even though you are here on Earth, having this life experience, you are never disconnected from source, from the divine, the all, God - whatever you would like to call it. As you progress, you receive blessings and help from the Source, your higher self, all manner of positive and benign beings. After you have lived your life and return to the higher dimensions, you bring all the knowledge you acquired back to source, where it is stored as a learned experience.

Your Purpose Here on Earth

There are seven basic reasons for you to choose to come to Gaia to experience a human life. As well as learning your soul lessons, you also want to contribute to the human condition in some way. The reason you chose for being here now might be one or more of these.

- **To bring new inspiration into the world and to create.** To make music, create art, write literature, express your unique self, and bring your interpretation of the world to others.

- **To nurture, protect and encourage.** To have beautiful loving relationships with other living beings and have the opportunity to care and show love.

- **To heal, soothe, and reconcile.** To help others and be of service when they need it, to be the person to lead someone to wholeness.

- **To act as a catalyst for personal and social change.** To lead others to a better way of living, to see unfairness, and to change it for the good of all.

- **To teach, to transmit higher wisdom and spiritual truth, to practice skills and social values.** To inform and teach the truth of life, to impart knowledge and hope to others.

- **To lead, inspire and bring enthusiasm and vision.** To be a leader for change, to show the way of love and truth using all kinds of media.

- **To create structures, to provide foundations to build on.** To introduce new technologies, new sciences, new insights into the possibilities of life.

Think about your passions and talents. What makes you curious and want to learn? What gives you joy and satisfaction? Which ways do you connect well with others? The answers will give you clues to help you gauge your purpose and start to incorporate it mindfully into your daily life.

The Earth Game

The Earth Game is what we are all playing. It was set up for us to experience duality.

What does duality mean? It means that there are opposites: male and female, old and young, one religion and another, one nation and another; in short, concepts that seemingly divide and separate us from one another. These ideas tell us that there is some difference between us and someone else, and that difference is a problem.

The whole of the Earth Game is a lesson for us to see past all those abstract divisions.

Most of you have incarnated many times before. You agreed to take on a part and the details of your life were spelled out before you incarnated. You knew that you would be disabled, or a politician, or a teacher, or an artist. Together with others, you created a reality to share and experience through your senses. It is all a dream, and you are in a matrix, inhabiting a holographic program that has the elements you have mutually agreed to.

For eons, you have been conditioned to accept what you see in your world, to accept the education system that prepares you for the stress of the working world. You are told very early on that there is not enough, that you need to compete with others for scarce resources, that you need to accept ideas that go against your natural instincts and intuitions. You are taught that the surface differences between us—race, religion, gender, class, colour—are insurmountable and that we are too different; we want totally different things. You are told to believe that these divisions are so massive that they overshadow the idea that we are all humans.

We are a common species; we all have the same basic needs (food, clothing, shelter, love, learning) that we satisfy in slightly different ways (which makes the world a wonderfully rich and vibrant place).

When you are in a state of competition with others, you are focused on getting what *you* want from the world. This focus keeps you distracted from what is really happening: the total control of the majority by a very small minority of beings. These are people of power; they want us to believe that there are not enough resources for everyone, that there are too many of us. But are there, really?

Could it be that a very small number of people own most of the resources: the money, the fuel, the food, the medicines, most of what there is? You all know that when there is a monopoly of a resource, the owners can charge any price they want for the things you need, and you are forced to pay. You have been conditioned to believe that you must spend the whole of your life working, afraid that you can't pay your bills, afraid that you will lose your job and have nowhere to live.

Now that many are awakened to this false reality, we can reject this overlay, this matrix, this compliance with and acceptance of their system. We will find that there is enough of everything for everyone. The wealth and resources that our beautiful Gaia contains will be shared amongst us, each to his or her need. In an awakened and enlightened world, people do not want to take more than their share; they have empathy for others because they know we are all one.

The Law of One

This law is a body of knowledge that was channelled by a group of beings called Ra (a kind of collective, rather than an individual consciousness). Ra has been in contact with Earth for a very long time, directly involved with the history of humans, in the first instance in Egypt at the time of the pharaohs.

The Law of One has all the answers for our understanding of the ascension process, or the "harvesting," as Ra calls it. It is a very large body of work, and because it is a question-and-answer format, topics are mixed. There are different ways of accessing it, including an online filter system, where you can type in the topic that interests you, and you'll be able to read all the references that have been written. It is a very important resource for us to use as we seek knowledge throughout our awakening.

According to the Law of One, the purpose of our existence is to expand our awareness and consciousness into higher vibrational frequency, so that we can go forth and experience all that there is and then return that experience to the source. The reward for incarnating in this life and succeeding in learning the lesson we have set for ourselves is rising into bliss and the light of love.

The message from the Law of One is to trust life. Know that everything moves in an upward spiral, and life gets better. Pay attention and strive to improve, to become stronger, clearer, wiser and more capable as you create your life.

Reincarnation

The concept of a spirit living more than one human life is our understanding of reincarnation. This notion has been held since ancient times, and many religions espouse the philosophy in slightly different forms. Some believe that there is a progression from second density (plant or animal) consciousness to a higher one, at which point the soul can escape the cycle of birth and death and can permanently reside in the higher dimensions. Repayment of the debt of karma is the prime driver in this view. Other beliefs around reincarnation involve more choice, with beings having a soul contract to learn to experience life from a different perspective and to learn different life lessons.

The Akashic Record

The Akashic Record is the recorded witness of all human events, words, emotions, and thoughts in all time periods, including what we currently see as the future. The word *akasha* means "upper sky," where these records are kept in the etheric plane.

Each soul has the record of all the incarnations on their journey to perfection. There is no judgement attached to any event or intent; it is simply a list and description of all that happened. Accessing your Akashic Record is done through meditation with the intention of reading and gaining insight into your current life. In your life there could be something you are afraid of or avoid, and you cannot discover the cause of this strong feeling from this incarnation. Your clear intention is to learn from the wisdom that you have accumulated in all of your past lives and apply it to this one. The Akashic Record is a shared resource, and we should not access records other than our own. We can expect an answer through intuition, a sensory sign, or a verbal or written message.

Your Expectations

You try to do the best that you can at any given time, and you sometimes fall short of your own ideals. It is often the case that you set yourself very high expectations because you want to please others and confirm their hopes for you, or it could be that you want to show them that they were wrong about something relating to you. It is a very useful exercise to examine your motives and discover what makes you value something or pursue a goal in life. Are you doing it for yourself or for someone else? How much do your parents or others contribute, either actively or passively, to your decision-making?

It is easy to be guided by your own expectations or those of others and almost be on autopilot through your life, moving from one thing to another, without much thought and without examining why you are living this way. Reflection is an important skill to cultivate, living your life in a more conscious way, more purposefully and intentionally. Awakening will help you to have more focus and direction in moving towards your target of ascension.

CHAPTER 5

Who Is Here with Me?

Your Relationships

The most important relationship you will ever have is with yourself. That may sound strange, but it is the basis of the relationships you can have with others. If you accept and love yourself, regardless of your mistakes and imperfections, then you can do the same for others. If you don't like yourself much, because you think you are too thin, or not as smart as others, or whatever, it means that you are making judgements about yourself, thinking that you are not enough, that there is a lack, that you are perhaps not acceptable. None of this is true; you are perfect, just as you are. When you love yourself, you understand others and love others as well. We are all doing our best, making our way through life, learning our lessons, and becoming the best person we can be.

You are on your own journey; it is just you, and another being can't know everything about you at all. Don't bend to what society wants you to be. Don't change who you truly are to suit others and to have them accept you. Be authentic and follow your heart. Show the true you by your actions; do what your heart and soul lead you to do. And don't let the words of others fool you and move you away from your path.

As you learn and grow, you get to a point where you begin to see yourself more clearly; you gain strength, authenticity, self-acceptance, and confidence. You open your mind to experiences and other people, knowing in your heart that they cannot affect the real you. Whatever good will come out of any encounters will help you on your way and provide you with a message, with a clearer direction, a clarity that leads you on towards your goal in this life.

When you regularly reflect on your relationships, it leads to insights about yourself. Asking yourself what you have given and what you have received will show the balance of power in the relationship and help you to redress any imbalance. Thinking about the troubles or difficulties that you have caused another will teach you about seeing through the eyes of others and showing empathy and respect.

Accepting Yourself and Others

When you accept yourself, you know yourself; you feel compassion and you can forgive failures and weaknesses. You become whole and can see the entire range of possibilities that you have and that others are capable of. You can also be your true self, embracing the fullness of our joint humanity and seeing the whole of this experience as acceptable.

You don't have to repress the parts of yourself that you don't like; you just acknowledge that they are there, that you have faults, that you do not always do the right thing, that you make mistakes. You don't even need to judge this about yourself; you merely accept this as being there.

If you can say, "This is me, warts and all," it means you can take the energy you used for defending yourself and your idealised perfect image and use it for something more productive. If you know who you really are, you can meet yourself with open arms and accept yourself entirely. You won't need to explain yourself to others, and you can then accept the shadow in them as well.

Your worth is not dependent on being perfect. You need to stop judging your mistakes so harshly. We tell our children that it is okay to make mistakes, and yet we castigate ourselves and others for doing the same thing as adults. Each mistake is a learning experience, an opportunity to discover alternative ways of doing things.

What We All Want

Every sentient being is looking for happiness, seeking to avoid suffering, and fighting their own battles with fear, insecurity, and self-doubt. They are searching for greater meaning, purpose, and connection. We are all awakening to the truth that we are in this together.

When every being is awakened, connection and unity prevails; love binds us all together, and we all move together into the light of source, having accomplished our tasks. You will treat everyone (and every living thing) you meet as if they were you, with love and understanding. This is the New Earth that we are looking for, the new paradigm for living in an enlightened way.

It is easy for us to imagine that energy, as the material from which all is built, can contrive many manifestations of the life force. We see the animal, plant, and mineral kingdoms as clear evidence of life here on Earth. But there is more. In this multidimensional reality we are part of, there exists all manner of beings that most of us simply do not tune into in our current vibrational frequency.

Operating within the field of consciousness are many who are here to assist us to reach our goal of ascension.

The Angels

Angels are nonhuman spiritual beings that act as the messengers of the divine source.

They have worked with humanity from the beginning, providing us with suggestions and solutions, sending warnings and energy, giving comfort and love, and working directly or through others to guide us throughout our lives. There has always been an awareness of angels within our shared consciousness; several religions have adopted them as part of their spiritual truth.

Angels were created and cannot die. They have no gender, although people have endowed them with certain characteristics that help to bind them to us in a personal manner. They are seen to have leanings towards healing or music or animals or technology or other pursuits. This allows us to call upon certain angels for our personal needs.

There are orders and ranks of angels, as described in religious texts, and this further classifies them for our convenience. The study of angels is called angelology, and it has many proponents. You have a team of angels working with you, from the time you were conceived. This was part of the soul contract details before your incarnation, and a guardian angel is always with you. You can call upon your guardian angel and others to help you with every aspect of your life, from safety to advancement to relationships.

The angels will offer wisdom through dreams and intuitive feelings; through others speaking for them; through symbols, the lyrics of songs, feathers, lights, and all manner of signs to offer confirmation for any decisions you are making. Repeating number patterns will also show you that you are on the right track.

You ask for help from the angels and then release your own control over the situation and simply trust that the right outcome will be achieved. Sometimes you get the strong feeling to do something; sometimes, you might feel dread about something you are thinking about doing. But you will always be given the guidance that you need for your highest good.

The Elementals

The elements of earth, wind, fire, water, and aether are used to explain the nature and complexity of matter. Elemental beings are living embodiments of one or more of these elements. The elementals are the spirits of nature, and their task is to take care of it, live within it, and sustain and renew it.

Elementals are the direct helpers of Mother Earth and clean up not only the pollution and poisons we physically damage the Earth with, but also the energetic negativity that arises from our discord, our profit-seeking, and our abuse of this world. Elementals raise the vibration of an area, which is why you feel relaxed and energised when you visit the countryside but often stressed and overwhelmed when you go to the human-made unnatural confines of a city.

Some examples of elementals are fairies, pixies, goblins, elves, gnomes, dryads, brownies, unicorns, dragons, undines, mermaids, and sylphs. Most cultures throughout history have stories about such creatures and their interactions with humanity. Whilst the story itself may be imaginative, the existence of a whole realm of creatures peripheral to our own is true. Connecting with the elemental kingdom is done through belief, by heart-felt interaction, especially gratitude for their work, and by demonstrating your love of nature in your care for the natural environment and for animals.

Channelling

Channelling is the free and benevolent giving of knowledge from a being of a different or higher dimension through a person in this dimension.

This being could be a spirit guide, an angelic being, a nature spirit, or a galactic entity. Channelling is somewhat like tuning into a broadcast from somewhere else, being on the same wavelength. The person through which the information is channelled can be in an active or passive state. The information received can be written as it flows into the receiver's mind, or it can be spoken out loud as they are in a trance.

The person receiving the message is in a relaxed and expanded state of consciousness and aligns to the vibration of a higher being to receive and then share the information. Mediums are people who practice channelling frequently, as they can be accessed more freely by spiritual beings. Such a medium can discern the vibrations of the message, knowing that it is given in the frequency of love and so vibrates in tandem with their vibrations and is acceptable to them. Any being that has the frequency of light and love is channelling a message of wisdom and is uplifting and assisting humanity.

Your Spirit Guides

A spirit guide will act in the same way as angels do, guiding and advising us for our highest good. The difference is that a spirit guide is a spirit who has experienced at least one incarnation on Earth and is at a level of awareness that can assist others in their journey at that point.

These guides have paid their karmic debt and do not really need to reincarnate, but in their love for all humanity, they decide to share their wisdom. Spirit guides are non-judgemental, compassionate, and loving. They know what it is like to have the problems of being human, to not know what your soul purpose was and to have to overcome obstacles of all kinds to become enlightened.

They respect your free will and will offer suggestions (but not solutions) to help you along your way; they are like a wise and loving friend. You may have different guides when you are at different ages; some guides help at a specific time with healing or emotional issues. Becoming a parent, forging a career, and other major life events can reveal your uncertainties and insecurities, and your spirit guide will be there at your side to reveal things to you, to assist you, and to comfort and reassure you.

Spirit guides can be accessed during meditation times and other quiet times when you connect with nature. Ask for their name and also ask to be able to feel their presence in some way. They will give confirmation that they are there and are ready to help you. You may encounter them repeatedly in dreams or visualisations, or they may manifest their answers through synchronicities such as repeated number patterns, chance meetings, song lyrics, or other ways of confirming your choices.

Galactic Connections and Disclosure

Our planet is part of a solar system, which in turn is part of a galaxy, and that is part of the universe. It is a big place. Looking at all the pinpoints of light in a galaxy, knowing that each of those could be a home for some kind of being, leads us to imagine the possibility of an infinite number of universal entities. Scientists have confirmed that there are billions of habitable planets in the Universe. It is only logical that we are not alone.

Contact with other worldly beings has already been experienced by countless people throughout time. Archaeology and artefacts from ancient civilisations have proven that we are an important part of the universe, that we have been visited by star beings, galactic friends, and non-terrestrials. Depictions of items that are clearly out of place for that time are found all over the planet.

Some people are of the opinion that we were genetically manipulated by galactic beings at an early stage in our development into homo sapiens. Others believe that right now, we live amongst other worldly peoples, most benevolent but some not. There is a very strong belief that a disclosure of such knowledge will occur at some stage soon to demonstrate to the world very clearly that all the sightings of UFOs, all the statements from people who have encountered such beings, and many of the sudden technological advancements we have made are confirmation of our relationship with beings from other worlds. There will be profound shock and then questioning as to why this information was covered up by governments and other agencies.

There is great interest from our galactic friends in the ascension process we are going through now. Many of them have had their own ascension process in past eras. Beings from constellations and planets such as Venus, Sirius, the Pleiades, and Arcturus, just to mention a few, are watching us with love and are willing to help us on an individual basis, if we ask. There are many credible sources of information about our galactic friends, and it is worthwhile investigating the topic to gain a clearer insight.

Star Children amongst Us

Star Children are children who have come to this world with a mission to help and guide us through the ascension process. These compassionate ones are connected to all life forms, are rarely competitive, sometimes have memories of lives before they were born (in this incarnation) and are often wise beyond their years. They ask the big questions and are not interested in materialism. Some may have what we would term extrasensory abilities.

Star Children demonstrate love and awareness through the way they live their lives, and they have been incarnating on Earth for decades, some now being adults. There are different types of Star Children (including Indigo, Crystal, and Rainbow), and they are grouped mostly according to the time that they were born.

Star Children have the power to heal; they are psychic and very sensitive. Many have been misunderstood and subsequently disengage from the 3D reality, as they find it oppressive and limiting, particularly in the education system. As we move more confidently into the ascension process, the role of the Star Children will become more prominent, and they will act as leaders and teachers for all of us.

Crystals of Gaia

Crystals are part of Mother Earth, which means that they are part of nature and therefore connected energetically to the world we live in. Crystals have the power to heal us and manifest our intentions. As energy beings, they vibrate with a frequency that can connect with our own energy. We use crystals in technology, recognising their ability to store memory. In the quantum world, they amplify our energetic healing potential.

Crystals will often choose you when you are looking for them, as they match your vibration through their colour or shape. Different crystals have properties that can help you with your abundance or creativity, with releasing negative energy, with protection and grounding, and with increasing your feelings of love and well-being. Recognising the beauty and power of crystals will bring an added dimension to your life. As part of Gaia, crystals connect you to the Earth itself.

Showing Compassion

Being compassionate is showing concern for the feelings of others, suspending judgement, and appreciating their perspective on a situation. Compassionate people have high emotional intelligence and can easily find commonalities between themselves and others. Being compassionate bonds and connects us with others, improving all the relationships within our lives.

Compassion looks like warmth and tenderness, shown through gestures and actions that demonstrate love for others. It shows empathy and understanding and a willingness to help. It also shows tolerance of others and sensitivity to their circumstances. Both the giver and the receiver of compassion benefit from the transaction physically as well as emotionally, with a lowering of stress and a strengthened immune system.

Being in Competition

When you truly understand that each person is part of you, competition will lose its attraction. You know at a deep level that there is enough for all, that each being is deserving, that it shares the same consciousness, the same life force, the same will to thrive and grow. You will be an enthusiastic cheerleader for the success of every being. Their success is your success because you are one.

The notion of competing with others was programmed into us from a young age. We were conditioned to believe that there was not enough, and if you didn't get in first, then you would miss out. In an enlightened world, there is plenty for everyone; there is no need to be first because you will be confident that others are taking only what they need, and you will do the same. People will be guided by their compassion and empathy, rather than their perception of lack and fear of missing out.

Connecting with Others

You spend your whole life making connections with other living beings. In the Earth Game, it is all about the connections, the interactions, the way you perceive and deal with the other selves that are existing at the same time as you are. In this game, you are learning and practicing how to see only similarities and not differences between us, loving all of nature, and demonstrating this love through your true, heartfelt beliefs and the way you act upon these beliefs. Believing that we are all part of the consciousness of the divine, it is easy to look with love at all the other aspects of this consciousness and connect with them deeply on every level.

Unity Consciousness

Collaboration is a strength of humanity; when we work together for the greater good, we do magnificent things. We achieve miracles.

We have, over the millennia, fallen victim to the notion that someone else will take care of things if we give them the power to do this. It probably seemed like a good idea at the time. We distanced ourselves from the responsibility we had over different aspects of our lives, thinking that it was better to relinquish this control because someone else knew better than we did. We were foolish. We gave away the power to heal ourselves, to learn what we needed to know for life, to provide ourselves with food that was nourishing, and to understand others and the divine without the intercession of another. We allowed ourselves to be manipulated by the media and advertising. We sought and accepted advice from celebrities and believed what we were told by political and governmental organisations.

Then again, as a sovereign being, you would be surprised to know just how much control you do have. The current matrix setup is all around us, and you share an energetic reality with humanity on the macro and the micro scale. As an enlightened being, it is important for you to consciously reclaim your power and not allow others to manipulate your reactions and your thoughts, whether they are individuals or groups.

Within each of us is the power to heal our part of the world. When you understand the notion that we are all one, you can look at others as other selves and know that we are powerful and self-directing. You can manage every aspect of your life without being told what is best for you. You know this already.

Imagine a world where we could be certain that each person would act with integrity and out of love for others. Imagine knowing that you would not have to struggle against anyone or compete with them for resources to live, where there was no need for you to be anxious or worried because your every need would be met, where people would live with the intention of being peaceful and doing no harm to any living creatures, that all would be allowed to exist without hindrance. What a world that would be.

CHAPTER 6

What Am I Supposed to Do while I'm Here?

Ascension and Dimensions

Ascension is a state of being. Of course, there are many different versions of what will happen when we ascend, some of them related to the idea that we go up, as in the real sense of the word. If you subscribe to the idea of a multidimensional universe, then it is possible to have different dimensions all existing together, but not necessarily accessible to one another unless you have the key, which of course has to do with energy and vibrational frequency.

The first, second, and third dimensions are always on the same plane of existence. The fourth, fifth, and higher dimensions can be attained when your vibrational frequency is higher. When you are in the fourth and fifth dimensions, you can still access the lower. The thing is, when you are in the fifth, you really don't want to go back there.

So, what are dimensions, or densities, as they are more correctly called? We can look at this from a blending of physical science and spirituality. There are similarities, and this again shows us that as a spiritual being, we operate within the laws of science. The definition of densities for physics is they are different aspects of what we perceive to be reality; for spirituality, they are our points of perception of the world. For our purposes, I have completed the density descriptions only to the fifth density, but there are higher ones as well.

Density Number	Scientific and Spiritual Interpretations
1D	The first dimension contains minerals, crystals, water and the Earth itself.
2D	Sentient beings such as plants and lower animals exist here. Instinct governs behaviour, and life is lived in the moment. The lower brain of humans, which maintains our body's life support, is in this dimension.
3D	Humans and the higher animal kingdom are 3D. We live in a time/space and cause/effect paradigm. As humans, we experience the world as a separate being and see each other as different in many ways, and these differences overshadow any commonality. We judge others and seek happiness outside of ourselves. 1D and 2D exist in 3D.
4D	This is the realm of the unconscious mind. Dreaming, imagination, intuition, and creativity exist here. We are beginning to awaken, and our attention shifts from material pursuits to gaining knowledge about and understanding of ourselves. We begin to apply a filter of love and compassion to others and how we see the world. We are bound by linear time but can manipulate it to some degree. As we expand our consciousness, we experience a higher energy vibration. We need to strive and practice to maintain this awareness.
5D	Linear time and space do not bind our consciousness; we can live in all times and spaces. We live in unity consciousness, seeing others as other selves, dropping our egos, and focusing on healing ourselves. We fully understand that love is the only true power and that we create our own reality, knowing that the universe is within us. We have the freedom to create new ways of thinking, being, and doing without any limitations, physically or otherwise. We can manifest the world that we want through our consciousness and intent.

The goal for us is 5D and higher, and we often move between 5D and lower densities, according to what is happening in our lives and how we are reacting to those circumstances. When we can continually stay in 5D, we have transcended our limited human existence and have ascended.

Your Reality

You see the world by looking at it through layers of expectations, beliefs, associations, fears and desires; through cultural, religious, racial, and gender filters. You have your reality, and others have theirs. We all see a different world, and what we expect to see, and experience is what will happen for us. This again relates to the quantum field, where everything is possible and what we desire is drawn to us.

Your impressions of the world pass through all those multi-layered filters formed from your upbringing and experiences. What is, is replaced by what you think it is, and simple reality can be clouded by alternate interpretations and sometimes by your personal hurt and confusion.

Your attention resides in two worlds—the subjective and the objective—and your mind will fight to affirm the validity of your own impressions. Think about how multiple witnesses to an incident will not agree on the details that they all saw. Sometimes, judgements and prejudices will cloud the facts, as you operate from your subconscious programming. Looking at others with the knowledge that they are like you, other souls making their way through life, will help you to see more clearly.

When someone speaks, having a message with an intention, you don't always hear what they mean to say. Being in a state of mindfulness when in conversation will help pick up the subtleties of tone and body language, and perhaps you will hear closer to what was meant.

You operate most of your life on autopilot, with the subconscious mind in charge. It not only takes care of your body functions; it also will take charge when you are not consciously thinking. When you have been driving for several years, for example, it has become part of the programming, and you don't have to think about it much anymore. Of course, you must pay attention to the roads, but if you are preoccupied with thoughts or strong feelings, then somehow, you drive from here to there without any conscious focus on the mechanics or the route.

While this is a good thing (because you don't want to have to use your mind to remember how to walk or to tell your hearts to pump blood) there is so much more programmed into you, particularly when you are in the first six or seven years of your life. During this time, people in your family told you in no uncertain terms about how to live and manage in the world.

They could have given you messages about lack and competition, about your self-worth, about differences between people, about your life chances or intelligence. If you grew up in a family where your self-concept was deliberately enhanced, where care and concern for others was highlighted and practiced, where you were made to feel that you were accepted no matter what, then you were lucky. Of course, there were also other influences such as the extended family, friends, neighbours, school, religion, the media, and so on. What you saw with your eyes, heard with your ears, and were encouraged to feel as emotions set you up for the rest of your life.

Going against the subconscious programming takes a lot of effort. Something in your thinking patterns that you do not like and want to change (for example, feeling like you are a victim) takes time and practice to overcome. There are techniques that can directly access your subconscious mind and reprogram it to new and more acceptable thoughts.

Brain science, especially that focused on neural connections, tells us that we are constantly making new neural networks with new information; and there is an ongoing pruning process that delinks old thoughts when we no longer believe those ideas. Regular and deliberate practices (mental, physical, and verbal) can override the old programming and deliver us into a more mindful, conscious, and enlightened way of thinking and living.

The Path

We humans like paths. We like the reassurance of going in the direction that others are going, and we like the companionship along the way. A common pathway confirms what we are thinking and tells us that at least one other person has had the same idea as we have and that is reassuring.

However, there are times when the well-worn path is not the way to go. As you awaken and become aware of the world as it is, you might face a harsh reality, finding that there are not as many as you would hope going along towards enlightenment. Some of the people who are the closest to you emotionally are rejecting (or at best just tolerating) what you tell them. You sometimes need to strike out on your own path and let the others go together, following their familiar habits and ways of living.

For you, that is no longer the way to go. This new direction can sometimes be a lonely one, and you may question yourself about making the right decision. The right path and the easy path are rarely the same. Remaining committed to your journey as a soul can result in personal struggles, but struggle makes you grow. Those who have failed to work towards their truth have missed the purpose of living, have not fulfilled their soul's purpose.

Today we find that many more people have started on their ascension journey, and they can be your company. There are countless communities online where there is mutual sharing and support, and we all love to hear that others are experiencing the same things that we are along the way. Humans are social creatures, and it helps greatly to know that we are not the only ones having such an experience.

Although these communities have the same general theme—awakening and ascension—their focus can be on different aspects. It could be that one brings together those who are interested in the galactic input of the process, both the negative and the positive. Another may be a forum for sharing ways of alleviating the physical and spiritual effects of the changes we are experiencing. Most will be a definite comfort to a lot of people, as they will be affirmed in their experiences and sensations. To know that others are feeling what we are feeling is a blessing.

The pathway to ascension can also be shocking. The process you go through as you discover the extent of the control that you have been subjected to can be daunting and even make you angry and resentful. But the lesson to learn is that it is what it is, and you can move on from that point in a positive and enlightened way. It is unnecessary to blame others and demonise them, knowing as you do that, they too were following their soul's plan. Be detached and focus on the way forward for yourself.

Your path, in some measure, has been set by the plan you had since before your birth, but your own free will always come into play, as you make the decisions that determine what happens to you on a daily basis. Every day is filled with small and large choices, with forks in the road to deliberate on, with possible scenarios presenting themselves for our confirmation or dismissal. Choice is always there.

Distractions in Our Lives

What everyone wants is happiness and peace; everything else is just stuff that distracts.

You may think that things outside of you will make you happy, but they don't really. You buy something because you think you will be fulfilled when you have it, but that feeling is very short-lived. Soon you want something else to fill the emptiness. When you have love in your life, things will come and go without you being attached to them; you will focus on your relationships and not on things.

When you are distracted from your soul purpose, you often miss the opportunities and the challenges that would move you along in your progress towards completion. You can sometimes disregard the little hints from the universe that take the form of people and songs and books and random conversations.

One of the most insidious distractions is the cell phone. Although generally useful, this technology has taken people away from what is going on around them into a virtual world, where connection through all kinds of social media is more important than interaction within the shared reality.

Take coffee shops, for example. If you went into a coffee shop a decade or so ago, you would have heard the buzz of excited conversation between friends. Now they are quiet, with groups of people staring at their cell phones. From the simple perspective of manners, the underlying belief that what might come through on a phone is more interesting than what might be said face to face around the table is quite telling. And quite sad.

Then there is the phenomenon of FOMO (Fear of Missing Out). The basic concept is that unless you are constantly connected, with messages of all kinds coming in, then you believe you are isolated and friendless, and your self-worth diminishes. Again, very sad.

Television, the box of programs sitting in a corner of everyone's house, is another major distraction from your real inner life. If you are a committed watcher of TV, then you may be comfortable with having other people with all kinds of agendas tell you how to think and what to believe. This is not only through advertising but through the news, which is filled with horror to keep you in a state of fear and often does not report significant events that don't fit the narrative of the mainstream media. It is important to carefully select what you and others in your family watch; minimising or even eliminating TV programming is desirable.

The Future (Not Really)

One of the hardest things for us to learn is to forgo worries about the future, to realise that your intention is out there, and the universe is busy working on the details for it to happen. We worry about those details, instead of just letting go and remaining in expectation of the fulfilment of our desire. Again, because time is not real, the desire is already in actuality; it already has happened. In the third dimension, we have linear time, and so it hasn't arrived, but in higher dimensions, it is there in its manifestation. You are living the life that you want. So, relax.

You spend your life trying, without much success, to control the variables: other people, time, events, and things. But if you can bring yourself to the point of not stressing about the details, the small stuff, and just have your thoughts on the overall prize, you can be more present in the moment and not have a cluttered mind.

If you are living through your heart, treating others as if they are you, and setting your intention, then the universe will take care of the rest. How the source decides to get you from where you are now to the place that you want to be is not your problem. Just put your intention out there, and let the universe take care of the details. As we are not bound by time or space in our energetic universe, anything is possible.

Paying Attention

Life is very busy for all of us, and it is important to pay attention. By this, I mean that you stop to reflect on the importance of what is happening around you and ask for guidance from your higher self. Very often, we go charging through our days, experiencing one thing after another, interacting with others, doing, doing, doing. Stop and just *be* for a while.

Part of our programming over time has been that we are always what is termed "productive." This was a guilt trip put on us, making us feel that every moment should be accounted for. We do this to children particularly, constantly structuring their whole day in the belief that they will make the association that being busy is the right way to be.

But it has all been a huge distraction, a societal overlay to keep us interacting with the shared construct and being outside of ourselves, instead of looking within and becoming aware of our great potential and our divine destiny. Take time each day to meditate and rest and nurture your soul, to take in the messages that were given to you that day, to absorb energy from nature.

Love Abounds

We are all filled with a never-ending amount of love to give. It is not a finite quantity, and no matter how much you give away, there will always be plenty more available. Give love freely. Be kind and loving, whether you feel like it or not. Feelings are important and are often an accurate indicator of what is happening around us. But loving practices are something that you do and not necessarily something that you feel.

When you speak with others, whether it is one person or many, speak through your heart; place your attention there, where the love is, and this love will go out with your words. When you look at someone, look through the eyes of love as you engage them in conversation. Bridge gaps of understanding with love. Connect your heart to your thoughts and send inner speech, healing wishes, and blessings to yourself and others. See from your heart. Listen without expectation, judgement, or opinions. This will not be easy at the beginning, because we are all used to looking at people and making a judgement about them. Try to look past all that to see the soul of a person.

View the world of nature and humanity with eyes of wonder and love. As your heart awakens more, your sense of separation and isolation begins to fade, and you will experience shifts in your perception of others, and then you will show this in the way you behave. The connection between you and all sentient beings will be clear and beautiful. When you love another living being, you are loving yourself, because you are them, and they are you. You will see others as members of the Earth family, without division or separation. There will be no difference between you and other humans, animals, plants, crystals, indeed Gaia herself. Life force is there. Love is there.

Being Kind

People always remember kindness. Even very young children recognise this as a desirable trait, and parents would do well having kindness as the one value to teach above all others. Kindness is a beautiful and powerful expression of the best of humanity. It is friendly and generous and warm and gentle. It shows people that they are accepted and supported, regardless. It rejuvenates the spirit and gives hope. Little gestures done from kindness are easy to do, and the benefits for both parties are amazing, so practice kindness whenever you have a chance.

Kind people act from a position of strength and self-confidence. Random acts of kindness, with no expectation of return, are a powerful way of spreading love and joy.

A respectful and kind mind-set enables us to be of service to others, improve our relationships and connections, and increases the general happiness quotient of the world.

Being Grateful

Be grateful for whoever comes into your life because each person has been sent as a messenger. In your life journey, you encounter so many people. Just think of all the people you have had contact with since your earliest memories: all the family members, the friends, the authorities, the random people you have met and interacted with in some way. Think about school, shopping centres, doctor's offices, bus stops, airports, the multitude of places in which you spoke with someone, sometimes long conversations, sometimes brief encounters. Many of those strangers had a gem of wisdom for you, something that you remember, some startling fact that affected you in some way.

It may have made you change your mind about something or decide to do something differently or to not go somewhere you had planned to go. They had that message; they guided you in some way. So, listen to what people tell you, especially unexpected and unknown people. They are there in the time and place that you are to tell you something valuable. Be receptive to the message. Think about it. What does it really mean for you? Who sent them with this message?

Be grateful for everything you are and everything you have. Wake up in the morning, and thank the universe for your warm bed in the safety of your house, for all the little but important details of your life, for your family, for your friends, for your teachers and advisors, for the fact that you are able to eat that day, that you can shower and have clean clothes. We all have so many blessings that may not be afforded to others. The amazing thing about being grateful is that the universe is keen to keep on giving us more when we appreciate what we already have.

To extend the notion of gratitude even further, be thankful for the ones who are teaching you a lesson that you needed to learn. Your soul contract may include learning to forgive, so somebody will do something that at first sight is unforgivable. It is hard to look at this and say it is a gift, but when you think about it, it really is. It is the gift of an opportunity to rise above, to not be attached to the hurt, to leave something that is happening in that moment and move onto the next moment, not dragging it along with you. Be grateful for this opportunity to get a big tick beside your name as a lesson learned.

Hawaiian peoples use a concept called *Ho'oponopono*, which is a process of attuning to others with compassion and forgiveness and thereafter letting go of any negative feelings. They use the phrases "I'm sorry. Forgive me. Thank you. I love you." It is not necessary to say this directly to another person, but to their spirit, releasing you from negative ties. It really works.

Showing Generosity

Everyone is valuable, is worthy, and can make a difference in this world. I am sure that you have heard of the concept of paying it forward, where a good deed, totally unexpected, is repeatedly passed on to other random people, becoming a chain of goodness that never ends. This way of showing your love through charity is a perfect way of bypassing feelings of owing something to others when they help you. In an enlightened society, as everyone is one energy, whatever is given to one is given to all.

Generosity encompasses so much. It need not be related to money or things, but you can be generous with your time, your compassion, your physical help, your teaching and mentoring others, almost anything. Being generous is an act of will. The spirit of generosity does not include feelings of obligation or duty to someone. It is a gift, freely given and without expectation of return.

Being Forgiving

One of the most important lessons humans can learn is to forgive. For all of us, from little kids through to adults, this is a very difficult thing, but it is profoundly energising if we can manage it. We all know the scenario: Someone does something that we find hard to accept. We may not even directly confront this person about this but will keep rehashing it in our minds, thinking of clever and cutting things to say; in our imagination, the other person will immediately apologise, and everything will be okay. But we rarely ever get to that confrontation point; we are stuck going over and over the event, feeling the hurt again and again, feeling victimised, feeling powerless, and feeling wronged.

Because this is happening in your mind, you are the one who has the control. Getting to the stopping point, the point where you are detached enough not to feel the hurt anymore, is totally up to you. The other person is probably unaware of what has happened, and even if they are, they are not concerned with your feelings. You must deal with those yourself. To forgive someone else is a gift to yourself.

It means that you no longer need to dwell on the event; it is not important, it won't hurt you anymore, and you can move on in a positive way. You may be able to face the people involved after a while, or you may even be able to let them drift out of your life entirely. Whichever happens, you can feel the inner peace of knowing that the event has no importance to you, and this is a great feeling.

Having Grace

Know the power of grace, the practice of allowing others to be what they will, of being kind, of letting go of things that are not meant for you. Having grace is being consistently dignified, respectful, and courteous. Practice graceful detachment from the words and actions of others. Don't let the world bother you. With practice, you can go through life without totally immersing yourself in total interaction with everything around you, just choosing to dip in sometimes and not to at others.

To maintain your inner peace and grace, try to be of the world but only in it superficially and temporarily. Move into a space of solitude when you can. This refreshes you and makes you ready to be part of everything again when you need to be. Never underestimate the power of alone time, the time when you can meditate and think and breathe, withdrawing and resting from the demands of everyday interaction. It is a time for reflecting on life lessons and coming to a point of understanding and integration.

Your Inner Peace

Inner peace is knowing how to belong to yourself without external validation. When someone talks about you in a negative way, whatever they say is about themselves. They recognise a fault and criticise you, but that is usually mirroring what they see in themselves.

For you, getting to that point where what is said, negative or positive, does not actually affect your own self-concept, and therefore your inner peace, is your goal. If you recognise that there is some truth in what is said, then try to change, but don't necessarily believe everything. If you allow yourself to be managed by the opinions of others, then you will not appreciate yourself, and your life will be filled with anxiety.

The opposite also applies: When something annoys you about others, it is usually within you. Acknowledge this and look to see what you are doing and how you could improve. Being detached from provocations coming from people and events will leave you maintaining a balance and patient demeanour.

Another area that relates to inner peace is taking responsibility and not blaming other people or circumstances. Again, being detached will put you on the road to a more balanced life. Know that you chose where you are now, and therefore you can also choose something better for yourself. You are always in charge, and there are always choices.

Your Morality

When you are a moral person, you can differentiate between what is decent behaviour and what is not. This means that you know and practice mutually acceptable actions in relation to others, and you have a code of conduct for the way you operate in the world. This code was derived from your family upbringing and influenced by your culture, your religious beliefs, and your understanding of what it means to be a good human. Values such as compassion and kindness, respect and honesty, integrity and sincerity, and notions of being co-operative and hard-working, forgiving and fair were modelled and reinforced through repetition from your earliest interactions.

Humans are by nature moral and ethical. You know, probably without anyone telling you, that you should not be violent and cruel. You see the effect of these actions on others, and it is abhorrent to your humanity. You condemn discrimination and other injustices.

Because most of us operate within this moral framework, it builds a system of trust between us. You know that if you walk down the street to the store, people will not bother you and will respect your right to do what you want. When something bad happens, mistrust erupts, and fear of others begins to spread. Unfortunately, when someone's trust in the predictability of others' conduct is taken away through some action, it is quite hard to restore.

This is where compassion, forgiveness, acceptance, and unconditional love come in. Trying to understand why somebody chose to act violently or to commit another offence is the first step (compassion). Then forgiveness and acceptance and love will complete the process. Remember that this is for *you*. Releasing another person through forgiving them will also release you from the pain of reliving the event, of holding resentment and anger, of not being able to move on with your life. It is a gift to yourself.

The Truth

Truth is an interesting concept. Although we regard it as a rock-solid commodity, along with the rest of reality, it shifts and changes. There really is no set truth, only your truth and my truth.

You see truth from your perspective, through all the filters of your mind. And it can be affected by your physiological or mental state at any time. In order to avoid complete confusion in the world, there are truths we accept without questioning. These could be called universal truths, and they usually are accepted because they are proven through time and experience.

You learn that telling the truth is an important way to build trust in your family. Children who are constantly lying will often carry that stigma with them for a long time and be disbelieved at school and beyond. Sometimes, having a vivid imagination and telling stories is considered lying, and whilst an amusing yet implausible account of what happened can be tolerated when children are younger, such stories are not accepted as they grow. Children will learn to say things that conform to what their elders expect; they will agree to the truth of someone else so that they can protect themselves. And white lies, those little fibs that are said so that feelings are not hurt, form part of our communication processes and are usually harmless, although trust can sometimes be eroded if used too often.

In spiritual terms, truth is a little less slippery. Admitting that something is happening and calling the attention of others to it, however difficult that may be, is part of growth and enlightenment.

Many people will choose not to listen, as it profoundly affects the foundations of their life. Truth isn't always palatable, but telling it is necessary. By the laws of free will, it is up to the individual to accept the truth or reject it. But change will come about when we reveal the full truth, planting seeds that change the world. So be the truth in terms of furthering the ascension process. Shine your light, and others will see it.

You Change and Grow

As your life progresses, you become accustomed to patterns, to familiar people, and to ways of doing things and you can sometimes resist going from the known to the unknown. In any given group of people, for example a family, there are lessons to be learned from one another, and when they are learned, we move on to the next set of people and issues to be worked through.

Of course, we maintain contact with families, but on a different level. Family is a great place to learn the early lessons of life. Families are messy, and the members of a family make a lot of mistakes that are readily forgiven. So much is learned in those years of family life, both by children and parents. We look through the eyes of love at our family, and we practice forgiveness and acceptance. It's an easy thing for us to do.

Then you move on to other groups to learn more lessons. People will be placed strategically in your life so that an experience you have agreed on can be encountered and mastered. This person may affect you profoundly, trigger you emotionally, and even make you question everything about your life. This is a good thing. Your reaction to this person will show how much you have progressed as a soul. If you complete the lesson, you don't have to repeat it with someone else.

Our lives are full of changes. From your very earliest moments, life around you changed, once you left the safe environment of your mother's womb. When you were a baby, you never doubted yourself for one moment. You believed in yourself, and you demanded attention from the world as your right. As you grew, you formed beliefs about your own capacity, comparing yourself with others. You looked at others and thought they did a better job than you, you could not do that as well, you were less than the perfect one you thought you were.

These comparisons led you to believe that you were not good enough in some measure; they led you out of confidence into a state of fear. You were fearful of failing, of letting yourself or others down. Your fears are often increased when others share them. But as you awaken, you can look past these fears, feeling unattached to them. You can look at them as guidelines for your own experience. Catastrophe may or may not happen, but you will push through the barriers to complete whatever task it is. Think about the mishaps you could have had when you learned to ride a bike. Some of these were your own imaginings, and some came from other people. But you learned anyway; you faced the fear and overcame it.

It is a good practice to keep on challenging yourself to grow. Don't get complacent; have exhilarating experiences such as fire walking, skydiving, mountain climbing or whatever interests you. When we place ourselves in situations like these, it puts us up against the "I can't possibly do that" feeling, facing natural fears and overcoming them. Growth comes from this.

CHAPTER 7

Who Is in Charge?

Guidelines from the Universe

The source wants us to be happy, successful beings in this earthly plane. To help us with this plan, there are some universal guidelines that are applicable in all circumstances. There are seven of them, and they encompass all areas of existence and interaction with others. Most of them are scientifically proven to be true for all states of being down to the energetic level.

Name of Universal Guideline	Explanation
Pure Potentiality	• Everything is possible. The full range of events, people, feelings, and possibility itself is always available. • Creativity abounds in all forms, and any wishes and dreams have the chance to come true.

The Flow of Energy	• Flow is a natural state for energy; it is constantly vibrating and moving as it goes into and out of matter. • Within the field of energy to which we are all attached there is a readily available abundance in the universe; to receive it, we give to others, we make it flow • We keep the flow going, a dynamic exchange that moves the energy along its path, making it accessible to all. If we try to stop the flow, control the flow, or not let it flow, then not only are we depriving others, we are depriving ourselves of unknown sources of abundance. • The trick is to set our intention to having what we need and just know that it will be provided for us in the normal course of events. The details are not important; how it happens is not important. • When you are in the flow, you can just relax and not be stressed about the providence of what you need to live abundantly.
The Law of Karma	• In the interests of clarification, karma is not a punishment from the universe; it is a way of reinforcing a lesson. Once the lesson is learned (that is, if you don't keep repeating the same thing), then the imbalance is redressed, and you can move on. • The lessons you need to learn are about how you respond to certain events and people. Which conditioned responses do you have? When someone does something you don't like, do you automatically go into an anger state? Do you forgive others when they have done something hurtful, or do you hang onto bitterness and resentment? • If you continue to have the same conditioned responses to these events, then the universe will continue to give you opportunities to show that you have learned the right path, and if you haven't, then a reminder will be sent, in the form of some kind of little accident with further opportunities to show you have learned the lesson will manifest.

The Effortlessness of Life	• Nature works best in a state of flow, just letting things happen easily, harmoniously, and without external control. • When you try to control, imposing what you feel is the right overlay, resistance will build, and the flow will be lost. • When you resist and bring in your judgements and preconceived ideas, blockages in abundance, in development, and in the possibility of love occur. • Situations that were in the process of being resolved are held up, and instead of being quickly completed, they persist, creating problems that did not need to be created. • Just let it all happen; observe without judgement, even if you think that you have some kind of stake in the issue. • Be cool and in a flow state.
Desire = Fulfilment	• When you want something to happen, when you have a stated and definite desire or intention; the very fact that this intention exists contains within itself the mechanism for it to occur. • This law sounds very complicated, but it has to do with the field of quantum energy, where what you expect to observe will be observed. • This relates to pure potentiality in the way that your intention triggers the transformation of energy into the thing that you want. • Science has proven that the quantum field is influenced by desire and intention, so when you believe strongly that something is for you, then (if it is truly meant for you) it will be created from the infinite potentiality of the energy universe.

The Law of Detachment	• There are some things that are possible for you to have and some that are not. For example, we would all like to win the lottery and be rich, but this will not happen to most people, as it does not fit into the life plan decided by us before we incarnated. No amount of wishing will make it happen in that case. • If it is supposed to happen, it will. Detachment from the outcome will give you peace of mind. So just set your intention, and then let it go. • Whatever happens will happen. • Feel gratitude for what you already have; this is super important. • Know that whatever you need will come to you in the perfect time, and you can just relax, get back into a flow state, and let it be.
Law of Dharma	• You have a purpose for being here. Going back to the reasons you chose to be incarnated on Gaia, you are here to fulfil this purpose. It could be that you came as a leader, a teacher, a healer, a creator, or an agent of positive change in any field of human endeavour. • It may well take you a long time to discover why you are here. But when you follow your passions, which may be evident from a young age, you often arrive at the point you were aiming towards, even subliminally. • Some of you know exactly what you want to be; others take longer to discover this. Usually the universe will line up a series of hints, gradually getting stronger, that will guide you along the correct path. • When you are not aligned with your dharma, you feel misplaced and unhappy. If you take a job where you cannot be the real you, this will feel like misalignment and you will feel a lack of interest and passion. • When you are doing what you came here for, you are in a state of flow, and you feel fulfilled and purposeful.

In summary, flow is. All can just be. There is an acknowledgement of free will for all, but also a knowing that we are of one consciousness, and love can flow unconditionally and without judgement. Be open to accept whatever comes; keep your vibrations high by simply being cheerful and laughing more. Take every opportunity to connect with positive souls and meditate frequently, and you will help maintain this flow.

Synchronicity will manifest with signs that you are on the right track, such as repeating numbers, seeming coincidences, unexpected meetings, bodily sensations, and feelings of peace and joy. Your intuition will ramp up, especially as you start to place more trust in it.

Reactions and Your Power

You are responsible for your own life. You must realise that, even though events may seem bigger than you, you *can* control how you react, your emotions, your actions, and your responses to people. When you recognise that you magnify and sometimes distort your reactions and your emotions, then you begin to have a more measured response to events, a response that keeps you in the bliss zone, rather than going into chaos.

Keep breathing; look past the event and the words and actions of others to what is really happening and what it really means. Think about the relevance of this to the larger scheme of things; think about whether it will be remembered later, tomorrow, next month. Put it into perspective. Of course, if people have lost their lives, it is important to be compassionate and sorrowful, but when the mood turns into punishment or vengeance, then that goes against enlightened beliefs. Someone may be directly culpable but remember that they had a soul contract to fulfil, as did the victims. Comfort people for their loss, but don't be drawn into revenge or vilification of individuals or groups of people.

React to what is in front of you at any given time. We know that time is a series of moments in the now; the past is done, and the future is not here, so all you can deal with is this exact moment. This very fact reminds us that dwelling on the past or being stuck in resentment or regret is useless. Whatever it was can be fixed and moved on from. Again, forgiving yourself, forgiving others, and releasing the event can help you to go forward and return to the eternal now.

Your Entourage and Superpowers

When you made your soul contract, you volunteered to come here to experience a human lifetime. And you are not alone; there are many other nonhuman beings here as well. You are always surrounded by angels, and intergalactic beings have been here on Earth for eons, watching the proceedings and helping you to achieve enlightenment and ascension. As your own vibrations become higher, you will be able to tune into their higher frequency. Think about how radio and television frequencies work. You turn the dial or switch the channel, and the frequency of the one station or channel you want is found amongst all the other possibilities.

There are many races that were like us long ago, and they themselves went through changes that took them to other places around the universe. They had their own struggles, their own tragedies, but they became more like the source and therefore were able to achieve what we would think of as supernatural powers. Powers such as clairvoyance, clairaudience, and clairsentience have been available to us, and we are now able to access them more readily as we progress. These gifts are ways of communicating with other beings, including those of the natural world. Other powers such as levitation, astral travelling, and tolerance of physical extremes can be found already in some individuals living today, although we need to really look to find them. Mainstream media is not interested.

Service to Self and Service to Others

When you start thinking that you are part of the big picture, you begin to go into a more awakened state. You are important as part of that picture, and you fit into the scheme of all that is, in perfection. And in this perfection and love, you serve others as they serve you. Imagine a world where you can expect to meet loving-kindness at every turn, where you can move with certainty through your life, knowing that you will be helped and supported, and you can provide that for others as well, where love is present everywhere.

Service is an experience of wholeness and fulfilment. We know that this is what we are meant to do; why we incarnated. We didn't come here to compete or take more resources than others. We are here to share the love and show the love we have. Service to self is, in effect, service to others, as we are all the same energy. So, to translate that into understanding, when you treat yourself with great respect and love, it is part of your service to others.

Ancient Wisdom and the Mystery Schools

As self-aware beings, we have always sought to make meaning of life. From the earliest historical records, we can see that the questions of "Who are we?" and "What is the meaning of life?" have been asked and answered in almost every culture. We know deep down that there is more than just being born, living and working, reproducing, and then dying. We know that there must be a spiritual dimension, that we are more than just the meat of our bodies.

In both the East and the West, mystery schools, beliefs, and practices have flourished, with adepts seeking knowledge that was undiscovered or even forbidden at that time. Major religions have adapted wisdom teachings from ancient times to their own credos. Many concepts have been recycled and remodelled, and the tiny germ of truth they contain is revealed to the believers as suitable for public knowledge, within the framework of dogma that the religion espouses.

Ancient wisdom tools such as the Kabbalah, standing alone rather than attached to any religion, can give insights and knowledge about the very deep connections within the universe through the tree of life. The rituals and practices of Kabbalah and other spiritual ways can give us structure and meaning to live our lives in a thoughtful manner, connected with the source, with every living being, and with the planet we live on.

The Internet and Learning

The internet, which has only been around since the 1990s as the World Wide Web, is a great benefit to humanity, connecting the world in a way not experienced in history to this point.

Using this resource means that people can educate themselves. It gives people anywhere in the world access to information that will help them to learn something new or improve their processes or adapt their ideas. It provides a platform to disseminate knowledge in a nonlocal and nontemporal way. Having a large library of books was once considered to be a mark of a learned person. Now anyone can be learned; all you need is a computer and a connection.

The internet has brought the world together in a way that we no longer need someone to tell us what is happening; as citizen journalists, anyone with a cell phone can report and upload the news, and we ourselves can interpret it our way, without the filter and agenda of some media giant.

Education can now be universal and less prone to bias and withholding of vital information. We can learn about what is, and not just what someone else thinks we should learn. The rise in the number of home-schooled children throughout the world is evidence that the strong desire to learn and the availability of online resources can result in well-informed and skilled students. It is also indicative of the fact that many people consider their education systems to be flawed and inflexible.

Of course, there is a downside to the fact that everyone has access to the internet and so can disseminate knowledge that deliberately deceives. One must approach some topics with caution, as misinformation does exist. Checking with several sources will usually help you arrive at the truth. There is also the need to take care with the selection of appropriate content for young persons. New users can be guided to use the internet safely to enhance and improve their lives.

Using Affirmations

Affirmations are short statements, written in the present tense and focusing on a particular trait that you want to improve within yourself. Statements can start with "I am ..." or "My ..." and are specific to you. You could say something like "My day is filled with love and joy" or "I am creative, confident, and capable." You may repeat these affirmations several times each day over a period. You could focus on a few affirmations at first and then add others as you see the need.

Affirmations are not only used in spiritual practice but also as part of the psychological process to alleviate stress and overcome any self-sabotaging thoughts we might have. Affirmations highlight positive thinking as part of the daily routine, and as they are repeated, they can empower you and reprogram any negativity at a subconscious level.

People use affirmations to create the reality that they want, bringing a future hope into the present. For example, something like "I have a perfect living space" or "My salary provides for all of my needs and wants" will bring into being the life that you desire.

Writing down the affirmations and putting them in prominent places so that the thought is reinforced when you see the note is another way of sustaining the belief that you are able to ask for and expect the very best life for yourself.

CHAPTER 8

So How Do I Become a Better Me?

Your Awakening

When it comes to the awakening process, it doesn't matter how slow you go, so long as you don't stop. Most people have been in the process for a long time, including myself, from my teenage years until now, which is literally decades. It was a massive focus for a while—the questioning and the thinking and the realisations and the enhancement of my abilities—and then I would again become entangled by the outside world and forget my progress. Thankfully, with the help of so many, incarnated and otherwise, I am learning more and becoming more of who I truly am.

The tipping point of humanity's awakening has been reached, and more of us are living in a state of love and caring for others, seeing past any supposed differences to the essence of our shared reality.

That is why you are reading this book: because you know. Control has passed from the few to the many energy beings. The transition period from 3D to 5D is a difficult time, as the controlling elites scramble for the last vestiges of their power and lash out in many destructive ways to make people think there are some people who still need to be controlled. The rise in the number of violent episodes around the world and the displacement of people from their homelands is evidence of efforts to destabilise and traumatise the world population. The elites desperately want to continue their dominance, but many us have had enough, and it is time for us to reclaim our own sovereignty.

Everywhere, people are rallying to stand up to governments and other institutions, finding better ways of doing things and pointing out the corruption and mismanagement of our funds. It is important for us to tell them we no longer accept that they know better, as it has been amply demonstrated that they do not. People want to put the love back into our institutions, to focus on the fact that these collective organisations are there for the benefit of humanity, not as a money-making scheme for a few.

Sovereignty and Your Will

All humans are sovereign, meaning that we have within ourselves capacities such as personal power, independence, and an understanding of our responsibilities to ourselves and others.

You already have what you need inside. You have only forgotten, or you may have believed others when they made you feel that you were lacking in some way. But you are not lacking; you can reclaim your power when you have the will to do this.

The will is like a muscle. Use it more, and it will get stronger. When you have decided on your direction, your goal, your purpose, then exert your will to make it happen. If this is not infringing your soul's mission, you will find that obstacles will appear as challenges for you, and your willpower will overcome them.

Throughout our lives we demonstrate our use of will to achieve our goals. You may have had a strong will to learn to swim; you overcame your fear of water, of drowning, of sharks, of people telling you about the danger, of everything. You just did it through sheer willpower. You kept practicing until swimming was natural for you. Appreciate yourself every time you use your willpower to accomplish something. You faced any misgivings you may have had, and you did what you intended. You become more of who you are and less of what others thought you should be.

Detachment from the World

If you have ever read about mystics and their presence (they are unaffected by the world, not hurried, not worried, not reacting to external responses), you will realise that this state is perfection. Achieving this state took dedication, to repeatedly step back from reaction to outside stimuli, to practice staying in the state of neutrality, to not let the world pull you in. It took years to get there, but they did it, step-by-step. You can as well.

You may say that those mystics are far from the crowd, the everyday, the pressing need to do things. And you are right. It is relatively easy for them to stay in a state of detachment and peace as no one will tell them to get up and go to work or clean the house or make dinner. These daily distractions, and more, are part of our existence in this 3D reality; they are things that we deal with and they seemingly cannot be ignored. These are the products of being in this world as a human. They are the interactions that bring us together, and they are important as such.

Apart from the physical necessities, we also have a lot of mental traffic that demands our attention all day. The monkey mind keeps us in a state of confusion, and it seems that you have only just dealt with one thing when several more demand your attention. So how do we detach? With patience, practice, mindfulness, and a lot of self-talk.

It is a deliberate act on our part to still the confusion, to know that there are enough linked moments of time to complete all that needs to be done. Just breathe. Allow your thoughts to drift across the screen without focusing on them. In a gentle and unhurried way, attend to those things that need to be done for the smooth functioning of your life. Keep breathing, keep patient, stay in good humour, filter out the unnecessary, and keep moving until everything is accomplished. There will always be time and energy, and the very act of doing it becomes a mindful moment for you, as you focus on completion.

Detaching from negative thoughts takes practice and desire. Question the truth of each thought; ask whether it will be for the greater good for yourself or others and reject it if it fails these tests. There is a lot of validity in self-talk processes, such as cognitive behavioural therapy. You can identify erroneous ways of thinking and substitute positive thoughts that help you to change the behaviour that is not serving you well.

Being Worthy

Create your own worth through your actions. Know that even though you may not feel kind or brave or deserving, you are, and as you act in those ways, you embody those qualities. You didn't earn this life; you were given it as a gift. You were provided with the opportunity to live and to grow and to learn the lessons of being human.

Know that you are worthy, worthy of respect and courtesy, worthy of abundance, worthy of health and joy and love. Know that this is true, and when you feel that you are being treated poorly, know that you deserve so much better. Teach people how you want to be treated. Accepting disrespect shows that you don't think you deserve respect. As you go through the process of striving for that perfect state of bliss and withdrawal from the chaos of the world, having the support of nurturing relationships will reaffirm your value and worth.

Similarly, affirm others every chance you get, as they are your other selves anyway. Acknowledging someone with a smile, a nod, a greeting, or a compliment is a kindness that can be very powerful. It can lift someone's spirits; it can tell them that they are worthy and lovable and loved. Acts of kindness are part of the concept of paying it forward, as someone who has had their day brightened by your act of affection will often pass that on to others, creating a wonderful ripple effect in the field of consciousness.

Enjoying Abundance

The universe wants to deliver more to you, to give you abundance. All you need to do is know what you want and take the first step towards getting it. We are often brought up feeling that there is not enough, that not everyone will get a share of everything, that unless we strive and struggle and compete, we won't get any. It puts us into a fear-based mind-set, telling us that others are out to get what is ours, that we must be ruthless and excluding to have what we need and want. This is wrong. There is enough. There has always been enough.

One of the secrets of manifestation is to put your desire out there and not worry about the details of how it will be achieved; trust the source, the universe, God, to make it happen. Relax and be in a state of gratitude for what you already have, realising that blessings have already been given to you and will continue to be given. Again, in the state of oneness that we are as energy beings, we are not lacking anything. Be generous with your happiness for others, as they are you.

Everything in the universe is trying to help you; the universe wants you to win. Joy and bliss are the default positions of humans, but unfortunately, as we are beaten down with life, we lose this surety and accept a lot less than we are entitled to. We must all try to understand the concept of worthiness, that we are permitted to be happy and to want ourselves to be in joy and at peace all the time.

This may be a difficult state to maintain when you are in the middle of normal life, with others around you pulling you away from bliss. It is a matter of constant reminders to yourself that this is where it is best to be. Leave yourself notes; tape them onto your laptop at work. Tell yourself to breathe, to be zen, whatever will remind you of that perfect state. Have a daily routine of spiritual practices that keep you in the now moment and keep you balanced.

Being in a State of Mindfulness

Meditation and mindfulness bring us back to ourselves, leaving behind the distractions of the world and returning us to zero point, to the beginning, to where there is no time or place. We are in a state of being and not of doing. Mindfulness brings us into the place of creation, the space of potential. In this exact moment, there is plenty of time; you are exactly where you are meant to be, and this is a place of infinite possibility.

Time is always now; this moment is renewing itself over and over, with new things in it. Each moment gives us a brand-new chance to learn. Focus on this moment and be happy. Be aware of what is happening right now, without wishing it was different. We know that the only time we can change is this very moment, so to dwell in the past or spend a lot of time dreaming of the future is not productive. If we concentrate our mind on this moment, we come into the space of no-time, linking to the field of conscious energy, where everything is possible.

Living Meditation

Your mind is an ocean of awareness through which thoughts pass. Random thoughts become whispers, moods, emotions, desires, and impulses; they subsequently go on to influence your behaviour. When you meditate, you can observe your thoughts and purposefully ignore them, and they lose the power to control you.

The essence of meditation is paying attention to the moment and allowing thoughts to drift like pictures across a screen. When you watch a movie, you engage with the pictures, but when you meditate, you consciously give those thoughts no validity, and they move away, one no more important than the other. You come to the infinite field of consciousness where all things exist in a state of potential.

Whatever you do in your life, you can only do one thing at a time well. Keep your attention on what is happening right now. If you are working or playing, focusing totally on the process, the feelings, the moment itself; then, that activity becomes a kind of meditation. Some people use gardening as their meditation; others take the time when they are showering to focus on the sensations of the water and the feeling of cleanliness and freshness. This is related to the mindfulness mantra of "Wherever you are, be there."

What are the benefits of meditation? There have been scientific studies on the effect of meditation on the body; it has been proven to have measurable and long-lasting benefits to those who practice it regularly. Meditation brings a sense of deep rest and relaxation on the physical side, and moments of stillness that balance activity. When we meditate, we practice detachment and bring our busy monkey minds some pause and some relief. We can access the deepest parts of ourselves and the healing consciousness of the field.

As we periodically distance ourselves from the constant flow of life, we gain insight into the nature of subjective thought, gradually obtaining a kind of filtering effect that could persevere to our overall benefit.

For some people, focusing on the world and its beauty, lovingly examining a flower, watching a bird, or gazing at a spectacular view gives the opportunity for appreciation and the conscious counting of the blessings in their lives. Some like walking meditations, strolling on their own along a beach or in a forest, just being in that place with no reference or thought of any other. They bring their mind away from the daily schedule and apply it to the moment, seizing that moment (*Carpe punctum*).

Astral Projection and OBEs

Astral travel is an out-of-body experience (OBE), where the soul separates from the body and moves around the universe. The OBE could be intentional or not. People who have a near-death experience often have the feeling of floating above their body. Some native cultures practice vision quests, in which the soul travels in search of something. Food and water deprivation can sometimes trigger an OBE, so fasting for a long period can aid in the process.

When we astral travel, we realise that we are not just bodies, that the real us can be detached from its suit and move on its own to go anywhere or anywhen, not just on Earth, but to enjoy the unlimited exploration of distance and time. There are some ways to consciously astral travel that involve lifting out of the body purposefully during meditation or climbing out of the body (again during meditation) by visualising a rope going upwards. The prime objective is to enter the hypnogogic state (half-sleep) so that you know it is happening and can remember it afterwards.

Using Chants and Mantras

A mantra is a melodic syllable or phrase that can be chanted silently or vocally. The chosen mantra will have a strong spiritual interpretation of love, truth, or peace, and the words are usually in the Sanskrit language. Mantras act as a vibrational prompt to our subconscious, shifting negative patterns of thought or action.

There are many mantras to choose from. For example, "OM" is the sound of the universe, bringing us into harmonic resonance at 432 Hz. Some people use OM to align themselves before meditation. Others will use it to soothe a crying baby.

Chanting, repeating the phrase over and over, keeps your brain and body focused on a single task and thus helps in the meditation process.

Dreaming and Lucid Dreaming

Dreams are images, emotions, and sensations that occur involuntarily during certain stages of the sleep cycle. Dreams have always interested people as they attempt to draw meaning that can be applied at a conscious, everyday level. Physiologically, dreams process the memories, emotions, and other information we have through the subconscious. Dreams can be organically caused by events during the day; nightmares are stress and anxiety woven into a scenario played out as we sleep.

Many books have been written on dream interpretation, and the images are often ascribed specific meanings. Some people have prophetic dreams or recurring dreams focused on unresolved issues in their lives.

Lucid dreaming is when you are aware that you are dreaming, so for you as the dreamer and the character in the dream, there is an element of control of some aspects. Lucid dreams usually happen during rapid eye movement (REM) sleep, when the brain is very active, but the body isn't, or in the boundary between wakefulness and sleeping. In lucid dreaming, you create a form of reality, as you can go on adventures and interact and then remember what was said and done within the dream.

Using Divination

Divination is an attempt to get an answer to a question or problem by using a ritual or object. There are many forms of divination that have been practiced throughout human history and continue to be practiced nowadays. Astrology, bibliomancy, cartomancy (such as using Tarot cards), using crystals to scry or gaze into, horoscopes, the I Ching, numerology, and palmistry are just a few examples.

Each of these methods use different items and different rituals; asking a question to focus the enquiry is usually the beginning point of the process. Answers can sometimes be obscure, and so a collection of the patterns of answers and their possible interpretations, and the appropriate advice, is often given in a guidebook.

The Languages of Light

The Languages of Light are a new way of communicating that has recently come into our collective consciousness. These languages are channelled through Archangel Metatron and are a nonlinear, multi-layered stream of information that could be angelic, galactic, elemental, or Earth-based.

There are many of these languages, each with a different frequency and source. If you can speak one of the Languages of Light, then you are operating at a higher frequency. Within each of the languages, there are codes—sound energy—that bypass the limitations of our mortal mind, increase our intuitive abilities, and act as a catalyst for our ascension. The activation codes create more light in our cells, and this light carries an enlightened consciousness. Again, it is an expression of quantum physics in that the entanglement of photons (as energy) stored in the field of consciousness happens as you seek the light through using the language.

The Languages of Light work at a cellular level, speaking directly to our DNA and enabling healing and balance. Wherever healing is needed in our bodies, wherever there are energy blockages in our soul or our physical, emotional, mental, or karmic selves, or our potential for manifestation, these languages can restore the flow. They can also help with our communication with our higher self and thus to the divine source. As our energy field is in a constant state of change, we may need different healings at different times, and the Languages of Light will act on the energy that needs attention.

Languages of Light do not need to be understood by us on a conscious level; they are understood by soul and subconscious. When you speak, you sometimes cannot translate what is said. Some people *can* understand, getting a kind of summary message without knowing the individual words. There is an increasing amount of information available now about Languages of Light, and it is worth researching to see if one of them resonates with you. To start speaking, just have the intention and then speak. If you are ready, it will be there.

Your Merkaba

As energy beings, we all have a gridwork of light and sacred geometry around us that radiates this energy and connects us with the field. This gridwork electromagnetically links our multidimensional self with the universe. The word *Merkaba* translates as "light, spirit, body," and the shape of this grid is made up of two intersecting tetrahedrons that spin in opposite directions, creating an energy field.

The Merkaba keeps energy flowing and balanced, and we can use it to expand into any spiritual dimension, connecting with higher realms and with all time. Through meditation, when our energy is flowing, we can focus on the shape of the Merkaba and start it spinning in its light, moving off through time and space to wherever we want to go. Some ancient drawings of chariots of the gods are depictions of Merkaba travel.

Your Image

For some people who are focused on the external, it takes a great deal of effort to maintain their image. If you can relax in the knowledge that you are perfect in yourself and not in comparison with others, then you are acting in an enlightened way. In terms of physical perfection, a lot of us think that there is something gross about ourselves, maybe our hair, or our bottoms, or our noses. But remember that this is just the current package. Accept yourself as you are and do what you can to maintain your health and vitality, and then present your best self to the world without reference to others.

As a human being, you contain all things. If you can accept and love every part of yourself, even those parts that you or others reject, then the way to accepting and loving others is enabled. You can be the entire range of possibilities, divulge to the world every part of yourself, and welcome the full scope of your humanity. You can have all the wisdom, the foolishness, the assertiveness, every aspect of you for the world to see and admire.

Illuminate Your Shadow

We all have a light side and a shadow side. The shadow side is the part of yourself you don't like; you deny, devalue, and disown. The shadow is made up of the things that don't fit in with the person you want the world to see.

It is more than just the bad aspects of yourself that you want to hide; those you choose to keep concealed are the ones you think don't fit into your current living circumstances. It could be that you want to hide your assertiveness and seem meek and obedient because those around you expect you to act in that way. It could be that being gentle and sensitive will make others think you are weak. You could be hiding your warrior qualities of strength and action or your vulnerability and compassion.

We all have these parts of ourselves, and they are equally valid human qualities. Being able to show the real you, the authentic you, and be accepted is the ideal. Fortunately, most of us are accepted within our families, and as we grow older, we find friends and companions who know us and love us for who we truly are.

How do you find your shadow? Be an observer of your words, your thoughts, and your actions, both when you are on your own and when you are relating to others. Note what makes you angry or annoyed about others. This is usually telling you that that aspect exists in yourself as well or that you are suppressing part of who you really are. Sometimes, your dreams and the symbols or characters in them are ways that your subconscious shows you your shadow. And of course, your higher self will give you ample opportunities to deal with your shadow in relation to others.

If you are hiding your true and authentic self because you think others might not approve of you, take some time to reflect on this. What are you denying about yourself? What are you trying to conceal? What would happen if you showed the real you to the world? Is it that bad? The patterns of behaviour that you reveal to people over time lead to expectations of predictability and familiarity. Would it be so shocking to those people if you were the real you? If they could not take the real you, is their friendship worth it?

What is Fear?

When you take action it will always overcome any fear that you may feel. Fear will hold you up, make you procrastinate, and keep you from solving an issue. But once you are doing it, and engaged in it, your fear will disappear because you are not thinking about what might happen; you are just experiencing what is happening. You are in the moment: a perfect place to be.

It is important to free your body of the fear of what might happen. Start with your thoughts. Question them to establish their truth. Are they founded in fact? Will that really happen? How do you know that she is thinking that? What evidence do you have that he did that? Your mind is a magnificent puzzle-solver and will often work overtime to try to link things together, even erroneously. Your mind is brilliant but not always accurate.

Fear is stored in the body as physical tension; shallow breathing is one of your body's automatic reflexes. It builds up carbon dioxide in the blood, and sometimes people feel there is not enough air for them to survive, which contributes further to the feelings of terror. Generally, if you are holding your breath, you are fearful. Breathe consciously and remind yourself to breathe deeply at least once an hour, so that you take in clear and clean air; hold it in your lungs and breathe out any toxins that may have been trapped. On that in-breath, you are totally in the moment. Breathing, *pranayama*, is a mindfulness technique that is easily put into practice.

Your soul is immortal, but your body can suffer pain, injury, embarrassment, shame, or rejection. Fear is natural. It serves you well in keeping you aware of danger. But it can also manifest itself as self-doubt, insecurity, lack of confidence, inhibition, and shyness. You can be nervous and twitchy because of your own imaginings of what might go wrong. This fear limits you and your capacity to achieve what you could achieve. You might put yourself in a kind of cage to keep yourself safe and avoid the things that might happen, holding yourself back.

Psychological fear is indirect, subjective, and symbolic. Perhaps you are afraid of what failure may represent: losing face, rejection, abandonment, ostracism, worthlessness, mediocrity or being seen as a fool.

To sum up, fear is a little like a bully; if you turn and face it, it will back down. Even strong fears like phobias can be released. There may still be some residual feelings, but you no longer let it control your actions. When you challenge yourself to face your fears, you change from "I can't do it" to "I did it."

Punishment

You all received moral directives as children. If you were good, you were rewarded. If you were bad, there would be punishment in store for you. It may have taken you years to understand, and then to comply with the code of conduct that was part of your upbringing, but you tried your best because of your inbuilt survival mechanisms.

When you grew up and left your family, you were free to act as you would like to, to do the things you had not been able to do when you lived at home. Some of you went crazy; others applied the principles learned as children to their new independent lives. They saw the sense of the rules, and because these had become part of their subconscious, it was easy to operate on automatic. For most of you, it was a bit of a shock when you realised that not everyone thought the same way as your family did and some behaviours were not universally acceptable.

As an adult you still make mistakes, but now, there may not be an authority figure to contend with; you might be able to get away with it. Strangely, though, you punish yourself if no one else does. Punishment will not be sitting on the naughty step or getting beaten or being verbally abused.

It will take the form of quitting and not continuing to try for what you want, of giving in to someone else, of seeking abusive relationships, of addictions, or of engaging in behaviours that undermine your health, your possibilities for success, and the relationships you try to establish. You will literally sabotage yourself, thinking that you don't deserve to have peace and happiness.

It is all about your worth, but not as others see you; as you see yourself. Your worth is not dependent on being perfect, so you must stop judging your mistakes so harshly and know that you did the best you could. You often fall short of your own ideal. Take responsibility and stop punishing yourself.

You choose where you are now, and you can choose something better. You recognise that you could have done something different, and you know that you can avoid repeating those mistakes as you continue to live in the moment. Remember that the past is just memories you keep alive in the present, and so focus on doing the best you can right now, in this moment. Do things to reconcile with others physically or go within yourself to visualise those you have hurt and ask for forgiveness. Forgive yourself too, as it provides healing.

The past and the future exist only in your mind. So, pay debts by being kind, not by punishing yourself. Trust life. Pay attention and strive to improve and become stronger, clearer, wiser and more capable. Know your worth and value as an energetic being who is loving, lovable and loved.

Final Words

So, there it is. So much, yet so easy to condense into a few concepts.

Consciousness. Energy. Love.

The process of becoming awake and aware has been going on throughout human history. And this history is not what you have been forced to learn at school; there is so much more than what is in the textbooks (another interesting avenue of investigation, perhaps). For millennia, humans have sought to define perfection and to strive towards its achievement.

The Law of One talks about a harvesting of spirits when they have reached the highest level of awareness, enlightenment and understanding of what their incarnation is all about. This harvesting may be an event where people simply disappear, are raptured up and away from the rest of the population, who are left wondering what happened.

It may be a New Earth that we enter as we leave the old Earth behind, along with those spirits still learning their lessons. It may be that we enter a completely different timeline where peace and love abound, and there is no conflict or selfishness or lack. It may be that we get to choose to go and live on another evolved and enlightened planet. It could be that we exist at the same time as now, only in a different dimension.

All these possibilities could be true. There are many opinions amongst those on their journey, and each of them has validity and a certain attractiveness. I do not personally know what will happen, only that something will. There may be trauma and cataclysm associated with the process, or it may be a peaceful transition. Again, I do not know.

Timing is another uncertainty. People become quite intense about their journey and want evidence and confirmation that their process is sound and that their desire for an end to their trials will be granted as soon as possible. Since 2012, when the Mayan calendar showed the end of the current age, there has been an exponential increase in the number of enlightened people, and more become aware every day. Spirituality websites such as Gaia.com, containing all kinds of information, are freely available for us to learn from and then to go on to evolve in our own way.

The fact that so many have become teachers and healers and give their time and energy without expectation of reward, is indicative of the transformation of thinking that is happening. Some of these people speak about immanent disclosure and a rapid unfolding from that point. Others project that it will be some time in the future that a form of ascension will occur. No one really knows.

All we can do is to keep on perfecting ourselves, learning, loving, connecting, and doing our best to ensure that we are ready for whatever happens.

Going within and seeking solutions there, rather than externally, is the best plan of action. As we are part of the field of consciousness, of all that is, we can access the answers we need. Recall that there is no reason to agonise over what will happen or when it will happen; it has already happened. Know that you as a spirit will go on forever, merging with the bliss and harmony of the source when you are done with your learning. You will meet up again with the spirits who are your soul mates and with whom you have spent a multitude of lifetimes, interacting in different configurations and circumstances. What happens to the current package you are in is not that important. Like all flesh, it will fade away, and the real you will still live on.

You are here to learn and to love. It is as simple and as complicated as that.

Keep on moving towards this goal, demonstrating your understanding of the life lessons you have undergone. You know that you have truly learned something when you are able to repeat the lesson and apply it to all circumstances. You can do it without hesitation on every occasion that it is needed. You can keep on forgiving all of those who do something you don't like. You can keep on being caring and compassionate, even when it is hard to do so. You can stop and reflect on your own well-being and take measures to keep ourselves in a high vibration. Keep the goal of ascension firmly in your sights, and work on yourself every day.

Think about what you have achieved so far, the level of understanding of the purpose of life that you have now reached. Some of you might say that you don't know enough, but that in itself is an indicator of your wisdom. Wise people will always think that there is more to know.

Be guided by your soul's purpose in what you want to learn, what you want to share, and what knowledge you want to spread to help other selves. You are exactly where you are supposed to be at any point of your journey. Be grateful to your guides and your team, as they have prompted and encouraged you to get here. Be confident in yourself that you will continue in the perfect way for your development. Follow your bliss; do what makes you happy and fulfilled. Reflect and forgive and move yourself to joy at every opportunity. Be grateful and balanced and patient and loving to others. Observe the duality without judgement, and just *be* sometimes and not do. Remain in a state of flow and connect to all possibilities. Be guided by love in all your dealings with other selves. Above all, know that you do not need fixing.

It is all good. It has always been all good, but we didn't realise it.

Now that you know, move in confidence and love to achieve the highest state of awareness that you can, to be the very best version of yourself. My wish for you is that you keep on learning, keep perfecting yourself as a loving, compassionate being who knows that they are part of the divine. Open yourself to the magnificence of nature, of possibility, of bliss.

Keep your vibrations high and live at the top of the scale in love and joy and peace.

Namaste!

Glossary

Angels. Supernatural, positive beings who interact with us, giving us messages and helping us on our earthly journey.

Beings. Sentient living entities at all levels (dimensions, densities), from crystals, plants, animals, humans, angels, and galactic entities, an infinite range of life.

Dimensions/Densities. States of awareness of life and connection with the source and with all living entities.

Higher Self. The eternal, conscious, intelligent being who is the real you. Your HS sees and understands at the highest level. It has a direct link with the divine.

Incarnations. Your series of lifetimes on Earth.

Soul. The essence of you, your character, memory, thinking processes, inspirations and emotions. Your soul grows in understanding as you experience your lives, gaining wisdom and coming closer to your higher self and the source.

Spirit. A point of consciousness in the sea of energy, an individualised intelligence, the essence of a sentient being.

The Source, God, the All, the Universe, the Divine. The highest entity that is the Creator of all.

Veil of Forgetfulness. The border between our earthly lives and eternity. It stops us from remembering what came before in our previous lives and lets us start from the beginning with totally free will.

Acknowledgements

So many teachers have contributed to this handbook. Like so many others, I have read widely and deeply, as well as sought visual learning through websites. I have looked everywhere at everything. Almost all of it has been a revelation and sometimes a shocking wake-up call. I genuinely and humbly thank those who have helped me along my way, and I mention a few of those many below. Forgive me if I have forgotten someone and thank you from the bottom of my heart for your timely wisdom. When the student is ready, the teacher will always appear.

Louise Hay and Wayne Dyer
Richard Bach
Greg Braden
Theresa Bullard
Deepak Chopra
Paul Coelho
Diana Cooper
Howard Cutler
Erich von Daniken
Dr Joe Dispenza
Dr Masaru Emoto
Khalil Gibran
Corey Goode
Steven Greer
Graham Hancock

Nassim Haramein
Esther Hicks
David Icke
Susan Jeffers
Michio Kaku
Dr Bruce Lipton
Bill McKenna
Drunvalo Melchizedek
Linda Moulton Howe
Carolyn Myss
M. Scott Peck
Pete Petersen
Jason Rice
Rupert Sheldrake
Emery Smith
Russell Targ
Eckhart Tolle
The Three Initiates (The Kybalion)
Randy Veitenheimer
Doreen Virtue
Jay Weiden
David Wilcock
My own spiritual team.

Printed in the United States
By Bookmasters